OUTRAGEOUS WOMEN OF THE RENAISSANCE

by Vicki León

John Wiley & Sons, Inc.

New York • Chichester • Weinheim • Brisbane • Singapore • Toronto

D1206226

TO MY LOVING SISTER MARY LOU WOOLDRIDGE, WHOSE OUTRAGEOUS HUMOR
AND COURAGE ARE THE EQUAL OF THE WOMEN IN THIS BOOK.

This book is printed on acid-free paper. ∞

Copyright © 1999 by Vicki León. All rights reserved
Illustrations copyright © 1999 by Lisa M. Brown
Maps copyright © 1999 by Jessica Wolk-Stanley
Published by John Wiley & Sons, Inc.
Published simultaneously in Canada
Designed by BTDNYC

No part of this publication may be reproduced, stored in a retrieval system or transmitted in any form or by any means, electronic, mechanical, photocopying, recording, scanning or otherwise, except as permitted under Sections 107 or 108 of the 1976 United States Copyright Act, without either the prior written permission of the Publisher, or authorization through payment of the appropriate per-copy fee to the Copyright Clearance Center, 222 Rosewood Drive, Danvers, MA 01923, (978) 750-8400, fax (978) 750-4744. Requests to the Publisher for permission should be addressed to the Permissions Department, John Wiley & Sons, Inc., 605 Third Avenue, New York, NY 10158-0012, (212) 850-6011, fax (212) 850-6008, E-Mail: PERMREQ @ WILEY.COM.

This publication is designed to provide accurate and authoritative information in regard to the subject matter covered. It is sold with the understanding that the publisher is not engaged in rendering professional services. If professional advice or other expert assistance is required, the services of a competent professional person should be sought.

LIBRARY OF CONGRESS CATALOGING-IN-PUBLICATION DATA
León, Vicki.
    Outrageous women of the Renaissance / Vicki León.
        p. cm.
    Includes bibliographical references.
    ISBN 0-471-29684-8 (pbk. : alk. paper)
        1. Women—Biography—Juvenile literature.   2. Women—History—Renaissance,
    1450–1600—Juvenile literature. I: Title.
    CT3232.L46   1999
    920.72'09'021—dc21   98–30357

Printed in the United States of America

10 9 8 7 6 5 4 3

C O N T E N T S

"On this day in history . . ." You've seen, heard, or read these words a million times introducing bite-sized bits about the famous names of the past. If you keep track of them—as I have—you will find that about 90 percent of the movers and shakers who get talked about are male. And the feminine 10 percent are mostly women born in the 20th century. Does that mean that our foremothers did little of lasting value?

No way! During nearly 5,000 years of recorded history female achievers have been on hand, making the world a more interesting place, often outraging their societies in the process.

This book focuses on the wonderful women who lived during the Renaissance era in Europe, which began around 1350 and ran into the 1600s. This vibrant age got tagged "Renaissance" (French for "rebirth") by art historians who wanted a word to describe the new vitality of the arts and the new popularity of the literature and culture from the ancient Greco-Roman world.

During these centuries, women and men had a fire in their bellies to explore the unknown—from faraway lands to ideas like humanism (which was more interested in the importance of each person than in religion). Creativity and learning flourished; so did conflicts between established religions, like Catholicism, and new ones, like the different varieties of Protestantism. In this era, women sometimes lost power they'd gained earlier. Women were also the main targets during the witch craze, which sent many thousands—including France's heroine Joan of Arc—to horrible deaths throughout Europe. Despite the odds, however, some of the world's greatest painters, strongest rulers, cleverest scientists, wisest thinkers, bravest heroes, *and* wildest outlaws lived and died during the Renaissance. What's more, they were women.

More often than not, the women who left their mark were lucky enough to have a brother, father, or other male mentor (an informal teacher) in the family. (On occasion, their talent left their mentors in the dust!) That was the case with Italian painter Elisabetta Sirani, who completed hundreds of works in her short life. England boasted brainy humanist Margaret Roper, personally taught by her father, Sir Thomas More, a famous thinker and political figure. Denmark had Sophie Brahe, scientist and gifted kid sister of the well-known astronomer Tycho Brahe.

Occasionally, women were mentors, too. Vittoria Colonna, a noted poet and religious thinker, was Michelangelo's best friend. She acted as a sounding board for his sonnet writing and his spiritual questions. In the New World, a young woman called Malinali was the key player in the Spanish victory over the Aztecs and other locals of old Mexico. Without her help at translation and tactics,

Spanish conqueror Hernán Cortés and his band wouldn't have survived, much less triumphed.

The Renaissance was also a peak time for female heads of state, including Elizabeth of England, Christina of Sweden, and Isabella of Spain. During her 45 years on the throne, glittering Elizabeth the First never lost her popularity. She left such an impression on her culture that a new term—"Elizabethan style"—had to be invented to describe the arts, drama, and architecture that flourished during her reign.

Quirky Christina of Sweden had an education to equal Elizabeth's—but went in a very different direction. A single ruler like Elizabeth, she stepped down rather than marry.

A married mother of five, Isabella nevertheless was the politically dominant one in her marriage to Fernando. She sponsored the first expedition of Christopher Columbus, which brought what we call the "Old World" and the "New World" face to face. This collision of cultures and new wealth gave the Renaissance additional momentum and scope. (Although books on the Renaissance traditionally focus only on Europe, you'll see several New World female achievers in this book.)

Other women exercised as much influence as queens—but often in rebellious or even secret ways. For instance, after Queen Isabella persecuted the Jews and drove them from Spain, a gutsy Jewish woman of wealth and compassion named Gracia Mendes set up an "underground railroad" from Europe to Turkey for her people, saving thousands from death. Fiery Irish leader Grace O'Malley was another rebel. Although Queen Elizabeth was determined to bring Ireland under England's rule, she couldn't help admiring O'Malley and her pirate tactics.

Not all achievers were blue-bloods. Common women of courage became icons. People admired, argued over, and even imitated women warriors of humble birth like Joan of Arc. Other commoners became famous writers and thinkers, like Sor Juana de la Cruz of Mexico.

Some Renaissance women gained fame for being major-league scalawags. In the seventeenth century, London's favorite career criminal was light-fingered Moll Frith. At the same time, the toast of Spain *and* the New World was a rambler, gambler, and multiple murderer named Catalina de Erauso (a former nun!).

Often the stories of these outrageous overachievers remain fragmentary, like a jigsaw puzzle with pieces missing. A surprising amount of data has survived, however—more than enough for us to get a good sense of their lives. Artifacts left by these women, from paintings to letters, also help us trace their achievements. The history of the fifteen women within these pages (and of hundreds of other Renaissance women, including the five whose capsule biographies you can find on pages 115–116) isn't set in stone, either. Researchers and scholars turn up new material regularly,

© 1993 U.S.P.S. All rights reserved.

archaeological finds produce new insights, and documents about women of the past, long thought unimportant, take on new meaning.

Because the female side of our past has been neglected in past centuries, people today rightly want to correct the situation. And that's what I'm after, too: a Renaissance or "rebirth" of our whole human history, one that includes and lovingly celebrates the lives and deeds of women this time around.

Part One

FRANCE
AND ITALY

FRANCE AND ITALY *The Renaissance bloomed first in Italy, and by the middle of the 1300s exciting new trends in art, architecture, and ways of thinking about the world had taken hold. Painters like Elisabetta Sirani and poets like Vittoria Colonna gained fame. At the same time, however, warring nobles—and even the pope—frequently fought over real estate and religion in most parts of France and Italy.*

Joan of Arc

(1412 - MAY 30, 1431)

She was a nobody from a French peasant family in little old Domrémy, population: 200. Her mother, Isabelle, and her father, Jacques, baptized her "Jeanne" or "Jehanne," but we know her better as Joan of Arc. She never learned to read or write more than her name. Swordplay and horsemanship weren't part of her world, but by the time she was sixteen, kings and generals would be amazed at her instinctive grasp of weaponry, riding, and military strategy.

Until her teen years, Joan led a quiet, ordinary life. She went to church and worked hard at farm chores, especially taking care of the animals. Like other French peasants, she worried and prayed for an end to the long war with the English, who for generations had been fighting to conquer France.

When Joan turned thirteen, everything changed. Heavenly voices began to tell her things, she said—voices that only she could hear. Several times a week, she had visions. Sometimes she smelled "heavenly scents." One day in the garden, Joan was hit with a shattering vision. Suddenly, standing before her, bathed in brilliant light, were Saints Catherine, Margaret, and Michael.

"You will become a warrior for God," they said. "Dressed in armor, you will help Charles, the heir to France, drive the English out of our land."

"But how?" Joan asked. "I don't know how to lead men into battle—or even how to ride a horse."

"Seek out the captain of the royal garrison in your town," the saintly trio told her.

And she did. At first the doubtful captain thought it was a joke. But Joan's sincerity and spiritual vision slowly won him over. He passed the word about this young prophet along to Marie and Yolande, the wife and mother-in-law of Prince Charles, commonly called the *Dauphin* (the king's oldest son).

"Bring her to the court at Chinon," the women said. As she waited for her audience with the Dauphin, Joan made friends with a young knight named the Duke of Alençon. He watched her ride horses and work out with a long lance like a natural. Impressed with her abilities, the duke gave Joan a warhorse of her own.

By now, Joan was following the advice of her voices. Most of the time, she dressed in the outfit of a young man. She wore a black tunic and jerkin (or vest), leggings with garters, a hat, and a sword. Joan also cut her hair, wearing it in the masculine fashion of a young page.

When she finally met with the Dauphin, he felt that Joan was genuine. A weak man, he was afraid to back her on his own, so he turned Joan over to several churchmen for examination. They held a three-week trial to be certain that Joan's mission was heavenly, not devilish. Satisfied, the religious leaders said, "She is a good, pure, and Christian person."

Now full of enthusiasm for his new wonder woman, Charles gave Joan 4,000 troops, a suit of armor that glittered like silver, and the title of *chef de guerre*—Commander-in-Chief of War. (During her life, however, everybody called her "*La Pucelle*"—the Maid. That's what Joan called herself.)

Riding with Joan were two pages, two heralds carrying banners, and a squire. Her personal banner was decorated with an angel holding a French lily called the *fleur-de-lis* in its hand. Joan also carried a sword—one she found quite by accident, buried behind the altar of a church.

In April of 1429, when Joan was 17, she confronted the English enemy. Leading her troops and archers, Joan rode towards the city of Orléans. She sent ahead the message, "I've been sent by God to drive you out of France. We will strike you, wherever we find you . . . "

Joan was no figurehead leader. The Duke of Alençon said, "All marveled that she could prepare artillery and draw up the army in battle order, just like a captain with 20 or 30 years' experience."

At the same time her modest behavior set an example. She slept in the field, alongside the men. Soldiers stopped swearing in her presence; knights and foot soldiers alike honored her.

When her army arrived at Orléans, now in its seventh month under siege, the French created a diversion so Joan could ride through the gate, her white horse and armor shining. It was late at night, yet people swarmed to greet her, happy at the Maid's arrival.

FRANCE'S FIRST FEMINIST
PRAISES FIRST HEROINE

Writer and journalist Christine de Pizan lived in Joan's day—about 1365 to
about 1430—and she witnessed the phenomenon of the teenaged warrior.
Not only was she an extraordinary woman of the French middle class who'd
made a successful career as a writer on feminist topics, Christine wrote the
only surviving account of the time about Joan. In it, she said: "What an honor
for the female sex, which God so loves that he showed a way to this great
people by which the kingdom, once lost, was recovered by a woman. A thing
that men could not do."

It took several battles for Joan's army to drive the 5,000 English troops into retreat. Although some of her generals tried to exclude her from active leadership, Joan was in the thick of the fighting, receiving an arrow wound to her shoulder. No matter; she urged more action. She wanted to keep the English on the run, pushing them out of the river towns along the Loire River, and freeing up the critical route to Reims, where Charles would be crowned as king of France. By early summer, thanks to Joan's persistence, the road to Reims was open for the first time in many years.

July 17, 1429, was a proud day. Joan, now known as the Maid of Orléans, stood next to her king as he was sworn in as Charles VII. "Now we must push on to Paris!" she urged the king. However, he (and his generals) preferred to make deals instead of taking Paris by force.

For her help, the new king asked Joan what he could do to reward her. "Lift the taxes on my village," she said. He did that, and made her family noble, giving them the surname of de Lys, after the lily of France that Joan had placed on her banner.

The next year, in May of 1430, Joan led a smaller army to defend the town of Compiègne. Halfway through the battle, the tide turned against her. She was captured by a mob of Burgundian French soldiers, greedy for the ransom of 100,000 francs that the English had put on Joan's head. In short order, the Duke of Burgundy handed her over to the English, collecting the coins.

The English imprisoned Joan in a tower at Rouen, interrogating her endlessly. They accused her of heresy (holding religious beliefs denounced by the Catholic Church) and witchcraft. In January, her 5-month trial began. Joan's main inquisitor was a bishop who hated her; he chose both the prosecutor and the 60 men who acted as jury.

Joan's voices had told her she'd meet with treachery. And she did. The French king now thought of her as a political liability, and he didn't lift a finger to help her. Although Joan defended herself ably, her trial was a political event, not a search for the truth. Its outcome was known from the beginning. At 7 in the morning on May 30, 1431, at the age of 19, Jeanne was excommunicated (officially thrown out of the Catholic Church), then burned alive at the stake in the old marketplace of Rouen.

Joan's horrible death went unmentioned in the writings of many European historians alive at the time. But the Maid of Orléan's fame had spread throughout the Mediterranean world.

FROM HERETIC TO SAINT IN JUST 489 YEARS

Some twenty years after her death, King Charles VII opened a new trial to overturn Joan's heresy and witchcraft conviction. It lasted for six years! Joan's mother Isabelle was among those who gave testimony to clear her daughter's name. The witnesses included a bitter enemy of Joan's, an English soldier who had laid a stick of wood on Joan's bonfire. Later (like the King of France) his conscience began to bother him. He admitted that as Joan died, "I saw a white dove flying away in the direction of France . . . and I am much afraid that I'm damned, for I have burned a holy woman."

But it took until 1920—nearly 500 years!—for Joan of Arc's reputation to be completely cleared and the Catholic Church to canonize her. Today she is a saint—and the most written-about heroine in all of history.

Her deeds shone brightly among the common people. The year she met her death, a squire to the Duke of Burgundy was traveling from France to Constantinople, the faraway capital of the Byzantine Empire (in today's Turkey). When he arrived, a crowd awaited. The people asked him, "Is it true that your duke captured the Maid of Orléans—and then turned her over to the English?" No one could believe the betrayals of the duke, the French king, and others in power, who let France's biggest heroine meet a gruesome, fiery end.

CHAPTER 2

Vittoria Colonna

(ABOUT 1490 - FEB. 20, 1547)

was poet
• friend of
MA
• was a
widow

Nearly everyone has heard of the great Renaissance artist Michelangelo. But how many know the identity of Michelangelo's best friend? Surprise—she was a woman. And a very different one, at that. But then, so was their long friendship.

When Vittoria met Michelangelo, she was a 49-year-old widow living at a lovely convent called San Silvestro in Rome. He was already in his sixties, the Grand Old Man of Italian painting and sculpture. The burly painter and Vittoria would often meet on the roof garden of the convent at 9 Via Maggio. Was this a secret romance? Not in the least. They met to talk about religion, poetry, art, and the meaning of life.

The two got to be friends around 1538, drawn together by their common interest in poetry. Vittoria had written verse since she was a girl. By the time she and Michelangelo became pals, she

was a serious published poet and the center of Rome's most exclusive intellectual group.

What we know of Vittoria's early life is probably typical of most upper-class Italian girls in the late 1400s. As soon as she was born, her father, Fabrizio Colonna, and her mother, Anna di Montefeltro, started looking for the best possible marriage for her (a business match rather than a love match).

They found quite a catch in Francesco d'Avalos, the Marquis of Pescara. When Vittoria was four years old, she was dressed in her finest velvets and silks for a formal ceremony of betrothal to the marquis. (Francesco was a mere child himself.)

Unlike many arranged marriages, Vittoria and Francesco connected, heart and soul. They wed in 1509, when Vittoria was nineteen; for two years, the couple thought they were in heaven. They lived quietly in the small seaside city of Pescara, the capital of the Marquis' lands.

In 1511, a war with France broke out in Italy, and Francesco rode off to fight. He and Vittoria wrote to each other often. Their letters were full of love, but they also spent a lot of time talking about the values they shared. For instance, in one letter she says:

"Your virtue may raise you above the glory of being king. The sort of honor that goes down to our children with real luster is derived from our deeds and qualities, not from power or titles."

The couple obviously expected to raise a family, but no children came. Vittoria prayed nonstop for Franceso's safety. Her prayers could not keep her husband alive, however. He fought war after war, was wounded in a battle near Milan, and eventually died from his injuries.

Vittoria felt like dying too. She ran away from well-meaning friends and family to grieve alone. She chose the small island of Ischia, just south of Naples, as her refuge. There she poured out her heart in religious verse. The poems she wrote, most of them about her husband, eventually grew into a book called *Spiritual Verses*.

Over time, Vittoria came out of her grief and made friends with several spiritual leaders. One of them, a Spanish humanist

---

VITTORIA'S THERAPY

In her lifetime Vittoria won renown throughout Italy for her sonnets, which she wrote to ease her sadness. Her deepest sorrow was her longing for her husband, the marquis—away on the battlefield, then absent through death.

You know, Love, that I never turned my foot
from your gentle prison, or freed my neck
from your sweet yoke, or tried to take back
all that my soul gave you from the first day.

named Juan de Valdés, got her interested in getting the Catholic Church back on a more spiritual track. Vittoria became a religious reformer. She contributed money; she visited convents and monasteries; she gave lectures; she debated with key people and wrote letters to them.

At some point, she found to her surprise that she was back in the everyday world. But it wasn't as idyllic a world for her as before. Much of Italy was now a battleground. Italian princes fought over nearly every inch of land. Their squabbles made it easy for foreign powers like Spain and France to invade and plunder. Even her beloved Rome had been attacked and burned by invaders.

Vittoria had grown to love the contemplative life. Entering the convent seemed natural to her. In Vittoria's day, convents of all sorts existed; some didn't require women to take holy vows of chastity, poverty, and humility. Her convent in Rome was one. She lived as a secular nun, wore street clothes, and had the freedom to come and go as she pleased. However, she still wanted to share intellectual and spiritual companionship with men—to have what we would call platonic relationships.

From her convent, she kept up a lively correspondence with many of the important men of her day. Among them were Pietro Bembo, church cardinal and writer on platonic love; and Baldassare Castligione, known for his famous book *The Courtier*. In it, he said that noble spirit, not noble blood, was the quality a man needed to be an ideal gentleman.

To him, Vittoria once wrote, "I do not wonder that you have depicted the perfect courtier, for you had only to hold a mirror before you, and set down what you saw there."

But the man she communicated with most of all was

Michelangelo. The two even corresponded when both of them were home in Rome, living right around the corner from each other.

Michelangelo wanted to be more than a sculptor and painter. He struggled to put his deepest thoughts on paper, in the form of poetry. To Vittoria, his mentor and sounding board, he poured out his feelings.

MESSY MICHELANGELO

This quarrelsome genius of a sculptor and painter fought with everyone—his father, his clients, his fellow painters. It's not surprising that he lived

alone. (Some historians believe Michelangelo was gay. He could have been, but it's hard to know for certain—he seems to have had very few relationships with men *or* women.) Although he had money and loved beauty with a passion, his place was a cold, dark mess. His personal habits were pretty grungy, too. Michelangelo avoided bathing, wore no socks, and smelled of goat grease from the cheap candles he used. He had few friends—but the few he had, he really loved. Vittoria was one. He saved all her letters. He even had 143 of her sonnets made into a book that he lent to others with pride.

PLATONIC FRIENDSHIP ON PAPER

Michelangelo's poetry wasn't nearly as great as his painting and sculpture. But it rings of sincerity, as in this excerpt from a sonnet to his friend Vittoria:

> To be more worthy of you, Lady, is
> my sole desire. For all your kindness
> I try to show, with all I have of art,
> And courtesy, the gladness of my heart.

Famous as he was, not many people got along with Michelangelo. He was quarrelsome, moody, and messy. Very messy. Vittoria didn't care. Her affection for him focused on his soul.

Although she may not have been a beauty, Vittoria also sat for Michelangelo many times. Some of the drawings he made of her still exist. In gratitude for her help and friendship, Michelangelo also painted three great religious works as gifts for her.

When Vittoria Colonna died on February 20, 1547, Michelangelo was there to say farewell. He kissed her hand, and later he said that he wished he'd kissed her cheek as well. People today sometimes claim that men and women can't be "just good friends." But the long-ago friendship of Vittoria and Michelangelo proves otherwise. Their friendship, based on mutual devotion and a passion for the larger truths of life, was as beautiful in its way as one of Michelangelo's paintings.

CHAPTER 3

Elisabetta Sirani

(1638–AUG.25, 1665)

She painted with such lightning speed that rivals and clients alike used to gossip: "Elisabetta must have had help . . . but from whom?" This young Italian teenager had no secrets, however. As a matter of fact, between 1653 and 1665, anyone could climb the stairs to the Sirani studio in Bologna, Italy, and watch her work.

Elisabetta's father Giovanni was a professional painter—a second-rate one. As a small girl, his oldest daughter would wander upstairs into his studio and draw. Giovanni paid little attention. After all, *he* was the artist and the male breadwinner in the family.

A bigwig local writer and family friend named Count Carlo Malvasia had the habit of dropping by the Sirani studio. An ardent admirer of the visual arts, Malvasia noticed the girl's precocious attempts.

"Look at her, Gian!" he said. "This child has a gift from God! It's up to you to develop her gift." Giovanni probably grumbled a bit; didn't he have enough to do, with a wife and three young daughters to feed? But Malvasia's urging worked. Gian began to teach Elisabetta about painting, from perspective to grinding colors. Like a starving person, Elisabetta gobbled up every bit of knowledge that her father possessed, then looked around for more. Soon her skill surpassed her father's talent.

By now, Giovanni saw that he had more than an artistic curiosity under his roof. Visions of fat fees and important commissions danced in his brain.

By the time she turned 15, when most normal Italian girls of good family were learning music, sewing fine seams, and flirting with boys, Elisabetta was hard at work. Monday through Saturday she could be found in the studio, working from dawn to dusk. The few moments she took for relaxation, she spent singing, playing the harp, or writing an occasional poem.

Her dedication paid off. She won a public commission from the city of Bologna to paint a huge scene from the life of Christ for a local church—the youngest artist ever to get such an honor.

STRANGE INSPIRATION

Until Elisabetta came along, Guido Reni was Bologna's most famous painter. He died in 1642, when Elisabetta was about four. Even if he'd lived longer, it's doubtful she would have studied directly with him. Eccentric Reni was phobic about women—he didn't allow any into his home, afraid of poison or witchcraft. After his death, however, Reni ended up next to a woman for eternity: Elisabetta Sirani. As Bologna's two most famous artists, their bodies lie side by side in a fancy tomb.

THIS WORK, CALLED
MELPOMENE (AKA
THE MUSE OF
TRAGEDY), WAS ONE
OF 150 PAINTINGS
DONE BY SPEEDSTER
SIRANI.

In addition to producing major portraits and large-scale religious paintings, while she was still a teenager Elisabetta opened a school in Bologna for other women of artistic talent. Before she set up her studio school, there was no place for Italian girls or women to learn techniques or have access to live models. Soon her studio filled with pupils, including half a dozen noblewomen and girls of promise as young as nine years old.

Two of her pupils were Siranis: her younger sisters Anna Maria and Barbara. They had talent in their fingertips, too. Both won commissions from local churches to produce altarpieces—an important honor. Judging by the lists of works they left, Anna Maria and Barbara probably were considered artistic successes until they got married.

By the time Elisabetta was in her late teens, this teacher-artist whirlwind had completed a very long list of paintings and etchings. Giovanni had good reason to be thankful for Elisabetta's talent. He suffered from arthritic gout in his hands. After a while, they were so crippled that he could no longer paint. Now his oldest daughter became the family breadwinner.

She turned into a local celebrity and then an international tourist attraction, painting with confidence and ease, often in front of visitors who were far more celebrated than she was.

Once she wrote in her notes, "On the occasion that the Duke of Mirandola passed through here, he came to see my works and to watch me work . . . as did all the princes and princesses, like those of Messarano and others, and all the important people who passed through Bologna this spring."

Elisabetta was at her peak as a mature artist by her early twenties. But the pressure from her father never let up. There were no vacations for Elisabetta, no boyfriends or talk of marriage in her future. As fast as she finished a work, Giovanni collected the payment for it. Elisabetta never saw any of the money. In fact, when she wanted to give someone a present she had to paint one! When Elisabetta's mother needed household money, her daughter would dash off a picture for her to sell secretly.

Many times, appreciative clients not only paid her but brought Elisabetta lavish gifts as well. Giovanni took these gifts also. He carefully stored them, only bringing them out when he wanted to show off to a prospective client. "Look—this is what the

---

FEMALE PAINTERS APLENTY

Two women made art history in Spain and Italy before Elisabetta was born. Much-praised Sophonisba Anguissola of Cremona became a court painter to the king of Spain and finished hundreds of canvases in her 93 years. Roman painter Artemisia Gentileschi, born 48 years before Elisabetta, died when Sirani turned 14. Her dramatic paintings, many on Biblical themes, won major praise. After they died, the works of these women were ignored for centuries. Now, however, Anguissola and Gentileschi (along with Sirani and other early women painters) are regaining their rightful acclaim.

CHRISTMAS
29
USA

Elisabetta Sirani, 1663
National Museum of Women in the Arts

© 1993 by U.S.P.S. All rights reserved.

Duke of so-and-so gave my daughter because he was so pleased with her painting!"

Elisabetta continued to paint at blinding speed. Her clients included the Grand Duke Cosimo III de'Medici. As her reputation grew throughout Italy and beyond its borders, a few sceptics still could not believe that Elisabetta worked alone. Surely she was getting help—from her father, from her sisters, from one of her pupils perhaps?

On May 13, 1664, the Siranis decided to hold a special "paintathon" at the studio. Working with a model, Elisabetta painted a complete portrait, from start to finish, in one day. Officials, wealthy men and women from elite families, and other big shots crowded into the light-filled room to watch her. Her performance stunned them. "Maybe now everyone will believe me," said the weary artist.

At the end of each working day, Elisabetta went to a small chapel to pray. But prayers weren't enough to keep her well. In the spring of 1665, Elisabetta woke up in pain. "It's only a stomachache, daughter," Giovanni told her. The pain got worse; she took to her bed. Giovanni got anxious. If Elisabetta stayed ill, how would she complete the paintings she was expected to do?

Finally she felt well enough to return to work. One of Bologna's biggest celebrations, Saint Bartholomew's Day, fell on August 24. Everyone had a day off—except Elisabetta, of course. She was busy on a painting for noblewoman Eleonora Gonzaga when her body exploded in pain. Somehow she wobbled downstairs, where she collapsed in her sister's arms. On August 25, she died.

Giovanni Sirani filed a charge with the local authorities,

claiming that a servant must have poisoned his daughter. (In that time and place, people often jumped to such conclusions.) After a long trial, the verdict came in: the maidservant was innocent.

The Siranis weren't satisfied. "We want an autopsy!" they demanded. The autopsy didn't prove or disprove the poisoning charge. However, witnesses at the autopsy saw a number of holes in the stomach of the young corpse. Today's experts believe that the 27-year-old phenomenon of Bologna most likely died of massive bleeding ulcers in her stomach and lower intestine. The stress of overwork probably killed her.

Elisabetta's father and mother were devastated. The people of Bologna and all of Italy mourned. The city came together for a memorial for its most famous female painter. In November, the Church of San Domenico was filled with flowery orations and music written for the occasion.

A local artist was chosen to build a catafalque—normally a temporary platform, made to hold the coffin during a funeral. Elisabetta's catafalque, however, was an enormous octagon, called the Temple of Fame, carved of imitation marble and porphyry. In its center, the grieving citizens of Bologna could see a life-sized statue of the young artist, doing what she did best: sitting at her easel, painting, with a smile on her lips.

Elisabetta left an indelible mark on the art world, one that is only now being appreciated. In the United States one Christmas season, millions of people even had an opportunity to own one of Sirani's works and admire it on a daily basis. How is that possible? Elisabetta Sirani once painted a wonderful Madonna and Child on an indigo and silver background; in 1995, that painting was selected to be one of the U.S. holiday stamps.

Part Two

HOLLAND,
SWEDEN,
AND
DENMARK

FOR MOST OF *the Renaissance era, the Low Countries (now known as the Netherlands, Belgium and Luxembourg) were ruled by the Spanish Empire. In the 1600s, the seven northern provinces won independence, with the help of colorful heroines like Kenau Hasselaar. (The richest province, called Holland, became the name that people most often called this new country.) In the colder lands of Denmark and Sweden, the Renaissance arrived later—and largely thanks to people like Queen Christina of Sweden, who enticed artists and thinkers from Italy and other lands, and Sophie Brahe, whose work on celestial bodies helped put Denmark on the map as a center for science.*

Kenau Hasselaar

(A B O U T   1 5 2 6   -   1 5 8 8)

To young Kenau Hasselaar, there was no better place in the world than her small Dutch city of Haarlem. In winter, she and her sister Amaron skated along its iced-over canals, tracing the silver branches that led to the trunk of the great North Canal. In spring, they went boating on those same canals. A few miles west of her home Kenau could explore the breezy shores of the North Sea, whose cold waters constantly nibbled at the low flat landscape. Kenau didn't know it, but she was living at the start of the Dutch "Golden Age."

Kenau came from a typical hard-working middle-class burgher family. Her father brewed ale and Kenau and her sister helped out at the brewery. When Kenau finished her cleaning chores there, she worked at home. A cauldron of hot water at her side, Kenau would scrub the front steps of her home, and the cobblestones of the street beyond, until they gleamed. Wednesday was

BREWSKIES FOR BREAKFAST

Kenau, like your normal Dutch girl of the sixteenth century, drank a hearty amount of ale with her meals. She even had a huge foamy mug of it for breakfast—the better to wash down her rolls and herring.

Beers were also brewed for festive occasions. At her "new baby" party, Kenau's parents hung a lace and paper "valentine" called a kraam kloppertje on the front door to announce her arrival. At the feast, her dad put on a traditional father's bonnet (shades of party hats!), then served the crowd a special brew called "crib ale."

With a population under 40,000, Haarlem boasted over 50 breweries. In the late sixteenth century, over 12,000 liters of beer were consumed every day of the year in the city!

the toughest—that was the day her mother, and every other housewife in Haarlem, cleaned the entire house.

Kenau still found time to wander the countryside. She never tired of the soft gray glow of the landscape, a favorite of the Dutch painters and engravers who crowded Haarlem. Above all, Kenau was drawn to the sea. She gazed at it, imagining the homeland of the Spaniards, many miles to the southwest. Their kings and dukes ruled her land. Kenau had a hard time understanding why these Catholic foreigners had the power to command Holland Province, where she lived, and other largely Protestant Dutch regions.

We don't know what sort of schooling Kenau had; much of what she learned probably occurred at home, working with a tutor. She got a good grounding in reading, writing, and arithmetic—

that's clear from her later work. Whatever the source of her education, she grew into a sharp-witted and spirited girl.

Girls in Kenau's day were gently but frequently cautioned to "dress modestly," "ignore flattering poetry," "avoid bold caresses," and above all, "don't go around town by yourself!" Dutch women of good family didn't usually marry until they were 24 to 28. Parents wanted their daughters to make a good match—one that wasn't just a case of "calf love," as the Dutch called it.

DUTCH DUDS

On Sundays, Kenau put aside her wooden or leather clogs and her everyday long skirts, patched and stained with workaday chores. For Protestant church services she put on her best clothes. Although the clothes favored by Dutch Protestants usually had dark colors and simple lines, Kenau probably wore garments of silk and a lace ruff around her neck. Underneath it all, she wore beautiful pantaloons and undergarments trimmed with the delicate lace of the region.

When Kenau was in her twenties, she met the man she wanted to marry. "Symons the shipwright, eh?" said her parents. This was a good match. Building ships was a worthy craft, and a booming industry in Haarlem.

So Kenau married her man. At the wedding, held around the year 1550, she and her groom shared a goblet of hippocras, the traditional marriage drink made of Rhine wine spiced with cloves and ginger. Soon Kenau had her new household set up and a baby on the way. In a few years there were four young ones.

Then the year 1561 came, bleak as dead of winter. Kenau lost her husband. Suddenly she was a widow at 35, with four children to support.

As a child, she'd rarely been told that she couldn't do things "because you're a girl." So to her the next move seemed logical—she would carry on her husband's business. Accordingly, the next year Kenau marched into Haarlem city hall. "I want to register as an independent shipwright," she said. A few eyebrows were raised. Dutch women were a free-spirited lot, speaking their minds and doing all sorts of work. Widows sometimes acted as investment partners in ship-building investments. But running a shipwright's business? This went far beyond the norm.

Directing her workers to build and repair ships proved to be the easiest part of her new business, Kenau found. First she had to win orders—and that was no piece of cake. The widow became an international business traveler. Traveling by ship and by carriage, Kenau slogged through nasty weather on rough roads to meet with suppliers for her vessels and to persuade clients to buy her ships. When her children asked where she was going, she was as likely to say "Sweden" or "Finland" as the neighboring city of Amsterdam.

She had to be as tough as shoe leather—and not just because travel conditions were poor. In this male-dominated industry, both clients and suppliers often tried to cheat her. Sometimes they pulled it off, too. But more often Kenau went head-to-head with them. In fact, researchers have run across legal records of some of the lawsuits she filed—and won!

As the years rolled by, Kenau Hasselaar began to win more than contracts for new ships. She won a reputation. "The woman is as sharp as a new blade," the knowledgeable traders would say. In time, other Dutch women ventured into international business and trading. The best of them might be complimented by comparison. "She's a real Kenau," they would say, nodding sagely.

Kenau was in her late 40s when the political and religious issues between Spain and the Netherlands came to a head. For years, the 17 provinces of the Low Countries, including Kenau's own Holland Province, had been chafing under the cruel and uneven rule of distant Spaniards, the Hapsburg royalty. At last, the Dutch Protestants began to organize and rebel. The Spaniards retaliated with further cruelties.

In 1572, the Duke of Alba and 15,000 of his Spanish troops began a siege against the rebellious city of Haarlem. The citizens were terrified; Haarlem could muster only 3,000 men to fight the Spaniards! As a loyal citizen of Haarlem, Kenau decided her business could wait. She and her sister Amaron organized a large

VERSATILE KENAU
WENT FROM
THE BUSINESS
WORLD TO THE
BATTLEFIELD.

force of some 300 local women. At her own expense, Kenau paid for light armor for her troops, admiringly referred to by the locals as "Amazons."

"What will we use for weapons?" her sister wondered.

"The things we know how to use best," Kenau replied. Legend has it that she ordered her volunteers to assemble a variety of items from their own households. Then she led them, armed with cauldrons, cutlery, and other domestic "weapons" of iron, to the ramparts of the city. From the walls, Kenau and her female troops poured boiling liquids from their cauldrons onto their attackers. (Some accounts say that Kenau armed her women warriors with more conventional weapons—swords, daggers, and muskets—and paid for them as well.) Brandishing swords, the two sisters also led charges against the Spaniards outside the city walls.

The siege of Haarlem lasted for seven long months; the Dutch war with the Spaniards, five years. Kenau and her female army became quite good at construction work. Whenever the enemy broke through the city's defenses, they jumped in to do the repairs. Besides being a well-to-do widow, Kenau had resources to draw on as a brewmaster's daughter. One of the men who fought left a diary, which notes that in the heat of battle Kenau treated the Haarlem troops to jugs of beer!

When Haarlem and the new Dutch nation finally won lasting freedom from the Spaniards in 1577, local officials honored their heroes and their heroines. Kenau became immortalized in plays. Her face appeared on many a patriotic woodcut and engraving. Luckily for us, a Dutch portraitist saw fit to capture her, carrying her sword and wearing her medal for heroism on her sleeve. The pragmatic Dutch awarded Kenau Hasselaar a further honor: as a pension for her old age, she was given the post of tax collector! Her name even entered the Dutch language. "Kenau" came to mean "a fiery woman"—the sort that helped carry the day in the siege of Haarlem.

CHAPTER 5

Sophie Brahe

(1556 - 1643)

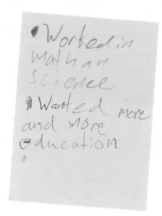

• Worked in math an science
• Wanted more and more education

In 1556, a girl was born to the Brahes on their fancy estate in northeastern Denmark. Sophie was the baby in a family of ten children. The Brahes weren't your everyday Danes of the sixteenth and seventeenth centuries. Sophie's mother Beate and father Otto never let their daughter forget she was of noble birth—and that everyone expected her to marry someone equally wealthy and grand.

Sophie wasn't a classic Danish beauty. When she looked into the mirror, she saw a girl with chubby cheeks and an almond-shaped face. True, she had a high forehead, a feature much admired in those days. But her mouth was a bit too small, her nose a bit too long, and her brown eyes protruded a bit too much for conventional prettiness.

But Sophie had more on her mind than her looks. She liked to tag after her big brother Tycho, the family genius who had been in love with star-gazing since he had seen a solar eclipse one summer. The summer Sophie was seven, her brother carefully made observations of the planets Saturn and Jupiter as they overlapped in the sky. Excited, he told his younger sister, "I'm right on target—but the record books are wrong!" That event transformed Sophie. Although she was still a child, she caught star fever too. She really identified with her brother—and he with her. Unlike their siblings, these two were crazy about science—and stubborn as mules about what they wanted.

Sophie would have gotten the normal education of a Danish nobleman's daughter—literature and music—but she insisted on more. Tycho jumped into the family fight. "Sophie's interested in math, philosophy, and astrology, too—just as I am!" he said.

The Brahe parents were hard to convince. Eventually, however, Sophie and Tycho wore them down. A succession of tutors just for Sophie began to come and go from the house. She couldn't wait to learn all they could tell her about classical literature, philosophy, mathematics, astrology, and alchemy. Even more, she loved the tutoring she got from Tycho, who returned home from school each summer.

When she was 15, Sophie's father died. Her brother, who'd finished his college studies in Copenhagen and Leipzig, came home to stay, and he set up a small observatory.

From him, Sophie learned how to identify and track planets and stars and document them on paper. She did this with her naked eye—the telescope wouldn't be invented until 1611. Then the most amazing celestial event yet occurred. On a chilly November night in 1572, when Sophie was 16, they witnessed a brilliant new star, located where no star should be. It was a supernova—a violently exploding star. Sophie was tremendously excited and proud. With her observations, she had helped Tycho predict this awesome spectacle!

To reward Tycho Brahe for his astronomical work, King Frederick of Denmark gave him a wonderful grant: the island of Hven. The King provided money, which, combined with Tycho's inheritance, paid for buildings on the island. Soon a fantastic three-story observatory began to take shape, with the grand name of Uraniborg (after Urania, the Greek Muse of astronomy). Almost everyone called the place the Heavenly Castle.

Sophie spent as much time as she could on Hven, where she was indeed in heaven. Uraniborg was a large complex, designed by the best Italian architects, lavishly fitted out with conference rooms, a library, and bedrooms for scholars and the occasional royal visit from King Frederick.

TYCHO'S NOSE

By 14, Tycho had already studied logic, philosophy, math, music, astronomy, and more at Lutheran University in Copenhagen. Then he was sent to a German college to study law; to keep him on track, Ty's parents hired a private tutor. By day, Tycho studied law. At night, while the tutor snored, Tycho studied the stars. A hothead, Ty once got into a fight with another student. This led to a nighttime duel in which Tycho lost the tip of his nose! Ever inventive, Tycho replaced it with a gold and silver tip of his own devising.

Sophie's favorite place became the library. There she worked with a five-foot celestial globe, which let her see the stars in relationship to one another. The room was dominated by a huge instrument called a quadrant, which stood by a window looking out to the night sky. The quadrant had two great beams crossing each other at right angles, with a movable arc between the arms. The arc was divided into "minutes" and "seconds" like a clock. As Sophie observed a star or a planet, she lined it up with the arc. Once she had its position, she did calculations to give it a precise address in the sky. One observation wasn't enough; under Tycho's direction she and the other scientists did them night after night.

Sophie could have kept busy and happy at this work for decades, but family obligations intervened. The Brahe family found Sophie a good match in Otto Thott of Ericksholm. A much older man, Otto was a highly eligible noble with loads of property in Skane on Denmark's eastern shore.

In 1577 they married. It was the year a new comet blazed across the heavens—and Tycho figured out, for the first time in history, that comets were heavenly bodies. Sophie was thrilled—but she soon had the down-to-earth matter of a baby on the way. She couldn't run off to work at the Heavenly Castle whenever she felt like it. Nevertheless, she kept up her reading and studying whenever she could.

Barely a decade after her wedding, Sophie found herself a wealthy widow. Her sadness lifted when she found that Tycho needed her help on a huge new project. He needed to find the positions of one thousand different stars, and catalog them in a book that would replace all prior star catalogs.

Sophie went to Hven and attacked the star catalog with

relish. With new energy, she also took up the study of chemistry, medicine, and horticulture. Before long she had a reputation throughout Denmark, and later outside its borders, as an authority on biology and plants.

She stayed on the island for months at a time. Its own little world, the island had 60 fish ponds, a year-round water supply, corn mills, a paper mill, and a printing press. With her interest in plants, Sophie reveled in the herb gardens, the lush flowers, and the arboretum, which held three hundred species of trees.

While on Hven, Sophie crossed paths with a fellow scientist named Erik Lange. The two fell in love. By 1590 they were engaged. At first their relationship sailed along smoothly. The owner of large estates, Erik had the same social status and noble credentials as Sophie.

Erik, however, was a fanatical alchemist. Alchemy, the forerunner of modern chemistry, was a grab bag of science, religious mysticism, and hocus-pocus. Erik poured money into his research. Then reality hit. He went deeply into debt and had to sell his properties, one by one. When he'd lost it all, Erik fled to Germany.

The fiancée left behind was stunned and angry, but life was about to deal further blows. King Frederick died, and his son didn't care much about the famed observatory at Hven. Tycho quarreled with him, the family, and almost everyone else—and in 1597 he lost his grant to Uraniborg and the island. To Sophie's utter dismay, Tycho had to abandon his life's work; now in his early fifties, with a wife and six children, he finally resettled in the faraway city of Prague, Czechoslovakia. Like a spent supernova, Tycho seemed to burn out. In 1601, Sophie's beloved brother fell ill and died.

At this low point, Sophie had little to tie her to home. She made a bold decision: she'd leave her luxurious life in Denmark and go seek her fiancé Erik—something that well-bred women of her day just didn't do. Despite family objections, she left for Germany. Sure enough, she found Erik; after a joyous reunion, they married in 1602. Sophie probably had reason to question her decision many times. Erik wasn't a practical man. Soon he frittered away his new wife's fortune, still seeking the elusive goals of alchemy. They couldn't look to her family for money, either— they'd disowned Sophie for following Erik to Germany.

Once again, the responsibility for running a household and paying the bills fell on Sophie's shoulders. She went to work at whatever paid. Sometimes she got hired as a wise woman for her herbal and medical knowledge, doctoring the sick who couldn't afford a regular physician. More often, Sophie made money through astrology, one of her earliest areas of study. She cast horoscopes for a living—just like Johannes Kepler, the astronomer who'd inherited the huge star catalog done by Tycho with Sophie's help.

She and Erik had a number of presumably happy years together before he died. After Erik's death, Sophie moved to the Danish seaport of Elsinore, where she lived to the ripe old age of 87, serene in her belief that she'd followed her own star, no matter where it led her.

CHAPTER 6

Christina of Sweden

(1 6 2 6 - 1 6 8 9)

If there had been supermarket tabloids in the mid-1600s, Christina would have been on their covers every week. A monarch who didn't behave, talk, or dress as a woman was expected to, she brought the culture of the Renaissance to Sweden.

Christina always marched to a different drummer. Her father King Gustavus Adophus, whose military know-how made Sweden a superpower, died when she was six. Her gorgeous, grief-stricken mother and a series of aunts and ladies of the Swedish court were left to raise the only child—or to try to raise her.

They wanted her to be a good Lutheran and a role model for the Swedes when she took the throne at 18. They also wanted her to marry her cousin, Charles Gustave. But rambunctious Christina failed to go along with most of their well-meaning plans.

She was so smart, it was scary. Although she was a princess and wasn't required to exert herself, she got real joy out of studies in higher math, astronomy, history, and philosophy—the tougher the better. Each day, she spent six hours at her lessons. On her Saturdays off, she rode and learned to fence and shoot. Her father would have approved.

Christina was also a chatterbox—not just in English and Swedish, either. At the age of six, she tackled German, French, Spanish, Italian, and Latin. By the time she hit 18, she spoke Latin as well as any intellectual in Europe. Then she took on Greek, Hebrew, and Arabic.

Her courtly circle of royal ladies and counselors had another problem with their queen-to-be. They couldn't make her behave in a ladylike fashion. Tomboyish and in perpetual motion, Christina rode her horse recklessly, gestured wildly, swore constantly, and laughed boisterously.

Although her mother had been a famous beauty, Christina

was remarkably plain. She had pop eyes, sallow skin, a hump on her right shoulder, and a big nose—and she didn't care. Most of the time, she refused to wear jewelry. Even worse, she wouldn't comb her long tangled hair more than once a week. Her clothes were a fright, often stained with ink because she wrote so much. As she got older, Christina took to wearing male clothing most of the time.

The common people of Sweden adored her, however. Christina's eccentric antics, her practical jokes, and her friendliness made her the "queen of hearts" of her time and place.

By the time of her coronation on December 8, 1644, Queen Christina was living up to her own personal philosophy. "A person should aspire to be not a copy, but an original," she wrote.

The young queen plunged into state council meetings with as much relish as she had taken up rifle shooting. Wearing the big floppy hat of a seventeenth-century Spanish dandy, she would ride from Stockholm Castle to inspect her warships and receive ambassadors from other lands. Gradually she got Sweden out of the Thirty Years' War, which had been raging across Europe since 1618.

During her first four years, she expanded trade and industry

THE THIRTY YEARS' WAR

From 1618 to 1648 a war raged, doing most of its damage in Germany but eventually involving almost every country and kingdom in Europe. When it began, the war pitted Protestants against Roman Catholics; as wars do, it grew, including political issues and power plays among the Swedes, the French, the Germans, and many other groups.

in her country. An advocate of staying in school, the queen greatly multiplied educational opportunities for the average Swede, and made it easier for women to gain an education. Her sponsorship got the first newspaper in Sweden published in 1645.

Shrewd as well as brainy, this hands-on ruler knew what she wanted: to show her subjects that she could successfully govern alone, without depending on a man. This dependence, she felt, was the fatal flaw of her sex. So it wasn't long before she announced to the world—and to her stunned council—"It's impossible for me to marry. And that's that." At the same time, Christina felt that the Swedish people needed to know who was to reign after her.

By sheer strength of character, and lots of political wheeling and dealing, Queen Christina got everyone, from complaining peasants to peeved nobility, to accept her plan. "My cousin Charles Gustave will be my heir and the next king," she announced. (More than a little intimidated by his cousin, Charles scurried to do her bidding.)

Christina loved risk and excitement the way some people love chocolate. On the eve of her political triumph, she wrote, "The news today threatens to engulf the world in a great tranquility; but I love the storm and fear the calm."

With these great events swirling around her, you wouldn't think Christina would have much time for cultural or artistic endeavors, but she adored art and books. Her goal was to outshine every royal in Europe (which mainly meant men, of course) as a collector and a patron of the arts and the intellect.

During the final years of the Thirty Years' War, as her armies mopped up, she instructed them to send back the best paintings, art objects, carpets, and books. A stream of precious artifacts soon filled her Palace of the Three Crowns to bursting. Before long, she needed a staff of librarians and curators to look after the contents.

The news of Christina's glittering court, nicknamed "the Camelot of the North," got around. Scholars and intellectuals from Renaissance Italy, England, and Holland stopped thinking of Sweden as the end of the world and began making travel plans. The queen invited the brightest minds of her day, including the world-famous philosopher Descartes. And they came!

Already a dynamo, Christina became a one-woman National Endowment of the Arts and Humanities. She commissioned ballets; she imported stage designers; she set up an academy that subsidized artistic and scientific endeavor. She corresponded nonstop with the biggest brains of Europe.

Noted French scholar Pascal even sent his new invention, a calculating machine, with a letter that said: "I was moved . . . by the union in your person of two qualities which fill me with wonder and reverence, namely absolute sovereignty and sound learning. . . . "

But Christina, who'd made it as sole ruler in a man's world, who'd achieved the educational and intellectual status of a man, who'd become the Big Cheese collector and patron of Europe, had another goal that was going to knock everything topsy-turvy. She longed for freedom. She was fed up with being the headliner, a royal who belonged to everyone and who dutifully followed the dogma of the Lutheran religion as a role model for the Swedes. She wanted to be what she never had been: a private citizen. So she kicked over the traces once more—doing it "her way."

On June 6, 1654, she abdicated the throne and saw the crown put onto her cousin Charles's head. (Some historians think she did so to head off a rebellion by the local peasants.) Content for the moment, she headed for Rome, taking with her the best of the treasures from her palace.

Being a Protestant hadn't satisfied her; she thought that Catholicism might. On the way to Rome, she stopped at Brussels to be received into the Catholic faith. She entered the city on Christmas Eve, arriving on a golden barge to the accompaniment of fireworks.

It took her the better part of a year to reach Rome, what with the ceremonial stops, and all that luggage. Being Christina, she went to see the pope with her usual splash. The pope was in heaven—kneeling before him was the daughter of a Protestant hero and a former queen. What a triumph for Catholic Europe!

For the next three decades, private citizen Christina lived in Rome, surrounding herself with Beautiful People, hosting the Great Names and artists of the day. But she was restless. She tried to return to power, angling for the thrones of Naples, Poland, and even Sweden when her cousin died in 1660. None of her efforts succeeded. She remained a private citizen until she died at 63. In a letter to her most intimate friend, Cardinal Azzolino, she said, "I shall never be virtuous enough to be a saint, nor infamous enough to pretend to be one."

Part Three

THE BRITISH ISLES

FROM THE MID-1500S *through the late 1600s, England reigned supreme in drama, architecture, and other lively arts, due to Elizabeth the First's patronage and largely peaceful rule. But the British Isles also boasted strong women of another sort, from Irish rebel Grace O'Malley to the outrageous Moll Frith. These times also meant religous strife, and England saw its part. Heroic scholar Margaret Roper saw her father die at the king's orders for beliefs father and daughter shared.*

Margaret More Roper

(1 5 0 5 - 1 5 4 4)

There were plenty of daddy's girls in Renaissance England. Margaret More, nicknamed "Sweete Megg" by her father, was one of them. Her father, Sir Thomas More, treated her more like a sister than a child. Thanks to him, Margaret would become one of England's premiere scholars in hard science.

By the time she was born in London around 1505, Margaret's energetic father was already a household name. Besides being a member of the English Parliament, he was a scholar, a poet, an author, and an attorney in his spare time.

When Sir Thomas wasn't busy writing a book, participating in a trial, or making a speech in Parliament, he and Margaret would take long rambles through the meadows and countryside around London.

Besides being fun, their walks were educational. Margaret often wrote down the things she learned at his side. "I like to teach my children the uses of common things," her father said. "To know,

WOMEN IN MARGARET'S DAY OFTEN COVERED THEIR "CROWNING GLORY" WITH HATS OR HOODS.

for instance, the uses of the flowers and weeds that grow in our fields and hedges."

Sir Thomas had a very offbeat outlook for a 16th-century English father: he was all for girls receiving the same education as boys. Because formal schooling opportunities for girls were meager, he hired a whole array of tutors to come to the More home. Each day, Margaret, her sisters Elizabeth and Cecilia, and her brother John got lessons in their domestic classroom. Margaret was the oldest as well as the most intellectually gifted of them. She was serious about learning and loved a challenge. Her list of classes included Latin, Greek, rhetoric (we'd call it "speech"), literature, logic, philosophy, and music. And she took a special shine to mathematics.

Whenever Sir Thomas was called away on business, he wrote long letters to his oldest daughter. In return, Margaret had to write him a letter every day. The only catch was—it had to be in perfect Latin!

By the sound of it, Margaret suffered from terrible migraine headaches. When she was in her teens, she became seriously ill. Her doctors thought it was a "brain fever" caused by doing too much "brain work." (Unfortunately, today's doctors know better—and that excuse just doesn't cut it any more!) She eventually recovered, probably despite the doctors' treatments.

When she was just nineteen, Margaret combined her knowledge of Latin, her command of the English language, and her amazing grasp of religious matters into one ambitious project. On her own, she translated Erasmus' commentary on the Lord's

Prayer from Latin into English. To do so, she had to read and completely understand the writings and thoughts of Dutch scholar Desiderius Erasmus, a man so brilliant that he was considered the Einstein of Margaret's era.

Soon a suitor came calling—a young lawyer from Kent named William Roper, who admired Sir Thomas More very much. When he saw the More sisters, he found someone else to admire—and to love. He and Margaret hit it off in every way. He loved her sweet, shy nature and her bold brain. In fact, his own studies paralleled those of Margaret and her siblings.

In 1525, the two were married. Even though she was a housewife now, Margaret became intent on mastering an exciting new subject: astronomy. Sir Thomas was so supportive that he paid for a special tutor for her. He knew that she had a husband who'd be proud, not jealous, of her knowledge.

As her own five children grew up, Margaret continued the More family tradition. She set up a classroom and hired two tutors.

"THE ORNAMENT OF BRITAIN"

A sixteenth-century genius, Dutchman Desiderius Erasmus stayed at the More house as often as he could. This philosopher-scholar was very impressed with Margaret's ability to move easily between classical languages and modern English. Among other things, he sent her a letter calling her "the ornament of Britain." The scholarship shown by Margaret and her sisters moved him to say, "The home of Thomas More is truly the abode of the Muses." (In Greek mythology, the nine Muses were the goddesses of music, drama, poetry, and other arts.)

With their help, she carefully taught her five offspring. She even included the promising daughter of one of the servants in her teaching circle. Her own studies were far from over, either. With zest, she now added physics and the Scriptures to her repertoire. She wrote poetry, orations, and essays in Latin. She translated religious and other works, and had them published.

In 1529, Sir Thomas became a favored advisor of the king, Henry the Eighth. But dark days lay ahead. Henry the Eighth met and fell for a commoner named Anne Boleyn. Unfortunately, he was still married to his first wife, Catherine of Aragon. In this Catholic era, no one—not even kings of England—got divorced.

Henry grew frustrated. To divorce Catherine, he needed people of importance on his side to help him sway public opinion. Who better than Sir Thomas More, one of the best-known and best-loved figures in English public life? Henry craftily appointed Sir Thomas to be High Chancellor of England, hoping to make points.

Sir Thomas had integrity. He refused to back the King's actions, and he wouldn't sign the Act of Supremacy that would make Henry the head of the new Church of England. On May 16, 1533, Thomas More resigned his office—the same month that young Anne was crowned as the new queen.

Margaret feared for her father—and with good reason. It was very dangerous to oppose King Henry. Soon accusations began to swirl around her father. One terrible day, the king's troops came to the More home and dragged her father off to the Tower of London.

For fifteen months, Sir Thomas was locked up. Margaret sent him long and frequent letters. He wasn't given any writing materials, so his letters to her were on scraps of paper, and they were written with a lump of coal!

Sir Thomas wasn't allowed any visitors, either. Margaret pleaded and begged, finally getting permission to see him. She lobbied for her father's release. In time, she made such a pest of herself at the king's court that she too was locked up for awhile.

The months wore on. In 1535, Megg's father was brought to trial. He was found guilty of being a traitor by the Solicitor-General. King Henry the Eighth had had his way. An important voice against him would now be silenced.

Her father was taken to the dock of the Tower, surrounded by guards. Margaret pushed through the armed men and hugged him tightly. Surprised and a little emotional themselves, the guards let her have a final moment with her dad. With tears on his cheeks, he

said, "My most dear Margaret, bear with patience but don't grieve for me."

Sir Thomas knelt before a grim figure in black who was holding an executioner's axe. In a moment, it was all over. For the next fourteen days, Margaret and her family suffered exquisite torment. During those two weeks, all of London could walk past the bloody spectacle of Sir Thomas's head, stuck on a pike at London Bridge.

Margaret still had the raw courage to make a deal with prison officials, who grudgingly allowed her to take her father's head down after that time. She had it preserved, along with her father's writings. And nine years later, when Sweete Megg died at the age of 39, her father's head was buried with her—her companion in death as he had been in life.

Elizabeth I of England

(1 5 3 3 - M A R C H   2 4 ,   1 6 0 3)

November 17, 1558, was one of the biggest all-day parties that England had ever seen. On that day, the unmarried daughter of the much-married King Henry the Eighth was crowned queen. Bonfires were lit throughout the land. Fireworks were set off. Proclamations were proclaimed. Groaning tables of food and drink were put up in the streets of London, so that everyone, common folks and uppercrust alike, could eat and drink and make merry for the new Queen.

At the festivities, tall and willowy Elizabeth Tudor the First dazzled the crowds with her red-gold hair, her regal air, and her warm way of greeting even the humblest citizen. A showy rider, she looked like an Amazon on her spirited horse. The common people loved her from the start—and it was a two-way romance that lasted 45 years. They saw Elizabeth as their protector. From them, she won the affectionate nickname "Good Queen Bess."

The little girl who would bring England into a Golden Age of peace, prosperity, and pride was born in 1533 in London. The first 25 years of her life read like a bad play, full of melodrama, murder, madness, plots, and prison. By her eighth year, Elizabeth had lost her mother, Anne Boleyn, and her stepmother Catherine Howard. Both were beheaded by her own father. In the next six years, Elizabeth saw King Henry remarry three more times, finally watching him get sicker and more crazy until he died also. Her beloved half-brother Edward reigned briefly, only to die of tuberculosis. A few years later Elizabeth even went to prison, locked up in the Tower of London by her half-sister Mary, then Queen of England and nicknamed "Bloody Mary" for her fanatical persecution of Protestants.

Despite all of this, the girl with the brilliant hair and the brain to match got an education worthy of her wits. Thanks to her governess and to Catherine Parr (the last of her stepmothers), she studied for two years with Roger Ascham, England's leading scholar, and had tutors for Latin, Greek, French, and Italian. In the mornings she read the Greek plays of Sophocles; in the afternoons she studied Roman writers Cicero and Livy, and read the New Testament in Latin.

Ascham bragged about his pupil, saying, "She's just passed her sixteenth birthday, and shows such dignity and gentleness as are wonderful at her age and in her rank. Her mind has no womanly weakness, her perseverance is equal to that of a man, and her memory long keeps what it quickly picks up."

KING HENRY THE EIGHTH: SO MANY WIVES, SO LITTLE TIME.

When she wasn't hitting the math or doing history homework, Elizabeth translated a book from French into English. Her idea of fun was to write daily letters to her brother—in Latin. An athletic girl with a keen eye for archery, she learned to dance, ride, and play the virginal, a small forerunner of the piano.

Once she became queen, Elizabeth showed her lighter side. She could be frivolous and flirty. She loved dancing—and not just the prim and proper kind. The First Lady of Style, Elizabeth also set the trends. She owned the most opulent dresses, the biggest lace ruffs, and the fanciest jewelry.

Over her decades as queen, she flirted often with the idea of marriage—but she never married. For years, she carried on seemingly serious talks about marrying this or that duke or ruler of Europe. For example, she toyed with a proposal from Philip the Second, Spain's ruler. Elizabeth had no intention of being the wife of a gloomy Catholic king. Meanwhile, she kept her country at peace with Spain. Later, she started a 7-year courtship with the duke of Alençon—this time, to keep the French as allies.

FASHION POLICE IN MERRY OLDE ENGLAND

Elizabeth and other rulers of the time often wanted to govern fashion. Many had regulations, called sumptuary laws, that listed the items that men and women of different social ranks could and couldn't wear. The lacy ruffs people wore around their necks, for instance, were regulated by Elizabeth's law. Hers, with 32 pleats, had to be bigger and more beautiful than anyone else's. She even had guards at the gates of London who were authorized to measure ruffs and cut off any that exceeded her law.

She also had a circle of wellborn English suitors who competed for her attention, men she favored as close personal friends. Even as an old lady Elizabeth expected flattering poems, passionate love letters, and chivalrous actions from her admirers. And she got them. Remember the story about Sir Walter Raleigh putting down his cloak so that his queen might walk with dry feet?

We might look at the horrible fate of Elizabeth's mother and the other wives of her father, and think: This woman feared marriage, and with good reason. But given the age she lived in, this "will she, won't she" diplomacy was an ingenious and workable way for an unmarried woman ruler to remain independent.

KNIGHTING SIR FRANCIS DRAKE— ALL IN A DAY'S WORK FOR ELIZABETH.

ELIZABETH—LUCKY IN WAR

When it came to her Navy's famous defeat of the Spanish Armada that came to invade England in 1588, Queen Elizabeth had luck on her side. Her ships, more maneuverable than the Spanish galleons, were just the thing for the weather, which turned out to be very English indeed. Three major battles took place in the English Channel and the North Sea. When the wind changed, letting many of the Spanish ships escape, the English had the last laugh. Huge storms capsized many vessels; only half of Spain's 150 ships reached home. Spain suffered a big loss of prestige, while England and its peace-loving queen showed that they could fight when they had to. As Elizabeth said to her troops, "I have but the body of a weak and feeble woman, but I have the heart and stomach of a king."

Good Queen Bess gave England three great gifts during her reign. The first was peace. Although she won fame for her fleet having defeated the Spanish Armada in 1588, she would do almost anything to avoid conflict. She was a very practical woman, and to her, war was mainly a destructive and expensive way for a monarch to throw her weight around.

Her second gift was that in 15 years Elizabeth reduced the national debt of England (sky-high after the reign of free-spending Henry the Eighth) to zero. This firm financial footing helped England become a world power. Her accomplishment is something that many American politicians today wish *they* could manage!

Elizabeth's third gift was her enthusiastic support of the arts and culture. The fancy poetry of Edmund Spenser and the splendor of William Shakespeare's plays were very popular. Just as popular, however, were the small books and pamphlets of the day, written in witty, sometimes racy street language.

How did Queen Elizabeth stay so close to her people? She went to them. She spent a great deal of her time moving around England in what were called "progresses." In those days, even the fanciest palaces and mansions got smelly and unhygienic after months of habitation. Most had floors covered with dried rushes, onto which everyone in the household threw leftover food, bones, and even grosser things. Dogs, rats, and fleas had free rein; bathrooms and sewers were primitive or nonexistent: perfect conditions for epidemics, in fact.

Progresses to newly "freshened" quarters became a popular way to escape the plague and other contagious diseases. (They didn't always outrun disease, however.) Elizabeth herself bathed and changed into clean clothes often—a habit considered most

BEAUTY ROUTINE OF A QUEEN

A strawberry blonde with milky skin and blue eyes, Elizabeth worked hard on her looks. For her skin, she used a bleaching lotion made of alum, eggwhites, borax, and white poppyseeds, among other ingredients. She had her own personal scent, a sweet and light aroma called "Queen Elizabeth's Perfume." Its main ingredient was the herb marjoram. She loved mouthwashes, too—and probably needed them. By the time she'd been queen for a while, her teeth were black as coal! Elizabeth kept her glamorously pale skin to the end of her 63 years; as she got older, her makeup got thicker, to cover her smallpox scars and the wrinkles of time.

peculiar by her contemporaries! Even with her habits, she did catch smallpox, and was very sick with it for a time.

Unlike our leaders, Elizabeth didn't take any trips abroad. The green hills and dales of England were good enough for her. For four and a half decades she moved about the land, getting to know her people and letting them know her. In doing so, she put such a stamp on England that her era was called the Elizabethan Age. It was the richest flowering of literature, art, drama, architecture, science, and exploration that England had ever seen.

CHAPTER 9

Grace O'Malley of Ireland

(ABOUT 1530 - 1603)

A free spirit, an outlaw, and an Irish spitfire practically from birth, Grace O'Malley lived a long and eventful life—as a pirate!

Around 1530, she was born at the family castle on Clare Island, Ireland. Her father, Eoghan O Maille, was chieftain of the Mayo clan. The little girl was named Grainne, which means "sun" in Gaelic, the ancient language of Ireland. When Grainne became a famous pirate queen, and the biggest headache the English had ever known, she got to be known as "Grace O'Malley," the English version of her Gaelic name.

Legend has it that Grace, the only daughter of the O Mailles, was born at sea. It could well be; the families of the Mayo clan spent more time on the water than on land. Some of their activities, like fishing and trading, were legal; others, like piracy, were definitely not.

In any event, Grace called Clare Island home. Her wild and lovely island was covered with a sprawling complex of fortresses and dwellings. It had fortified harbors around its edges, all designed to prevent surprise visits and to protect the clan and their wealth.

On their island, Grace's family kept flocks of sheep that fed on the windswept grasses. Clare Island also was a favorite nesting place for birds. Once, when a number of large eagles began picking off new lambs, Grace put on her hunting gear and went after them. As the story goes, during the fight an eagle raked the young girl across the forehead with its sharp talons, leaving scars. But this proud tomboy didn't care.

When Grace was six years old, things changed drastically for the Irish. Instead of being a free country run by independent Gaelic clans, each with its chieftain, the entire island was claimed by King Henry VIII for England.

PIRACY—A LIFESTYLE CHOICE FOR MANY

For generations, the Mayos and other Irish clans had intercepted ships traveling from Spain and England to rob them. Whether you called them privateers or pirates or buccaneers, this lifestyle was common for centuries among many coastal peoples, not just the Irish Celts. The rulers of Spain, England, and other lands officially condemned piracy; in practice, they often overlooked it, or even used it themselves. For example, Grace's English counterpart, Queen Elizabeth, turned a blind eye to buccaneers—as long as they worked for her!

The Irish clans made war with one another constantly, which made it easier for the English to gain ground. Soon, one clan after another had taken the bait offered by the English—such as special privileges and titles—if they would adopt the Anglican religion and English customs. The Mayo clan, snug on their secure island headquarters, stood firm, however.

Grace, who could sail a ship from the time she could walk, was already her father's pride and joy. Although she had a half-brother, Eoghan O Maille saw Grace as his natural heir. He groomed her to take over the clan's fleet and fortune. She was barely a teen when she took the wheel as captain of her first vessel.

Her role as leader didn't mean she was to stay single, though. When she reached 15 or 16, Grace married the O'Flaherty next door. A feisty lad, nicknamed Donal of the Battles, her husband was the heir of Donal Crone, the leader who ruled all of Connacht, a chunk of Ireland that made the Mayo lands look tiny.

Married and before long the mother of three, Grace continued to captain ships, make raids on vessels, and lead an active, seafaring life. Often with her toddlers on board, she ran both the O'Flaherty and the Mayo fleets. (Donal had his hands full on land, keeping peace among the unruly clans of Connacht.) At one point, Grace commanded over 200 fighting men and three raiding ships. It was a hard, unglamorous life, but Grace loved it. Tough as her men, she cut her hair short, wore scruffy clothes, handled a cutlass and pistols with ease, and played cards like a fiend.

Grace also did legitimate trading missions along nearly the entire west coast of Ireland and made longer voyages to Spain, bringing spices, wines, and other goods back home to sell. But when it came to pirate raids, she ruled the seas. It was rumored that she'd buried more than nine tons of treasure, taken from her raids of other castles and clans along the Irish coast. People nick-

MARRIAGE, CELTIC STYLE

Until the English imposed their more rigid laws, Celtic women in Ireland enjoyed many marriage rights. Brides who brought an equal amount of property as their husbands to their marriage were called "women of equal lordship." Husbands could not buy or sell their wives' property without the women's permission, as they could in other countries.

named her "Queen of the West." Soon she controlled five of six castles in Clew Bay.

The Irish pirate queen of the west was riding high until 1558, the fateful year that her English counterpart, Elizabeth, became queen of England. Right away, the English made big new changes in Ireland. They managed to overthrow the leader of the O'Flaherty clan; that meant that Grace's husband Donal was no longer next in line. Then the English followed up with an attack on Donal's own fortress.

Flaming mad, Donal and Grace fought the invaders. In the battle, Donal was killed, but Grace kept on fighting, and she won.

Grace didn't stay a widow long. In 1566, she married another chieftain named Iron Richard Bourke, whose family could point with pride to being the founders of Galway, an important Irish port.

The two lived in Richard's fort, called Rockfleet Castle, the sixth and key fortress on Clew Bay. With Richard, she had another child. Never a stay-at-home mom, Grace may have given birth at sea between raids. At any rate, her new son got dubbed Tibbot of the Ships.

By now, Queen Elizabeth herself knew all about Grace O'Malley—-and she was seriously worried. The pirate queen was the most formidable and tenacious fighter that the English had been up against. Queen Elizabeth, who was no softie herself, put a bounty on Grace's head. She also sent troops to storm Grace's castle. It was a failure.

The battles between England and Ireland continued for another twenty years. Grace, now the head of the Irish rebellion, won some—and she lost some. At one point, she was captured and spent nearly two years in a Limerick prison. Her husband Iron Richard died of natural causes in 1583.

When the new English governor for Connacht arrived on the scene, he hated Grace with a passion, calling her "a nurse of all the rebellions in Connacht." His first act? He took her son Tibbot hostage!

By 1593 Grace was tired, and her son was still a captive. So she made the long voyage to London to meet directly with Queen Elizabeth. What a summit that must have been as these two, both sixty-something but sharp as tacks, sized each other up! Grace saw a dazzling peacock of a queen, alight with jewels and gorgeous silks, a great ruff setting off her red hair, stark white makeup, and snapping eyes. Elizabeth saw a woman even taller than she was, an athlete with flyaway hair and weatherbeaten skin. Grace may have worn her clan colors of yellow and green, her only "jewels" a silver clip for her hair.

Queen Elizabeth served Grace tea. The two spoke a few words in Gaelic Irish, then got down to business in Latin, their common language.

The female summit got results. Elizabeth wrote an insistent letter to her Irish governor, demanding that he quit harassing Grace and give her a pension. As her part of the bargain, Grace shrewdly told the queen that she would make sea raids for the English—a promise she had little intention of keeping. For a short while, both women got what they wanted.

But further rebellion boiled up in Ireland, with Grace in the thick of it. In return, the English massacred thousands of unarmed prisoners. Grace herself got captured, and was only a few hours from death when her own son-in-law helped her escape.

The Irish kept on grimly battling the English until 1601, when they met with a final defeat at Kinsale. Heartsick and getting on in years, Grace retreated to her castle. The pirate queen died in 1603, the very same year as her royal English counterpart, Elizabeth.

Grace O'Malley is still a household name in Ireland, and the subject of songs, books, plays, and films. In the New World, the deeds of Grace O'Malley live on in another way. Each year, at dozens of Renaissance Fairs and Living History reenactments across the U.S. and Canada, you'll find women proudly playing the part of Grace O'Malley, Ireland's greatest pirate queen and freedom fighter.

Moll Frith

(A B O U T   1 5 8 9   -   1 6 5 9)

Merry olde England was still basking in the glow of its great victory over the Spanish Armada when Moll Frith was born about 1589 in a poor part of London called the Barbican. The records aren't clear, because Moll went by several names. In her line of work, aliases could be useful.

Tomboy Moll preferred to hang out with boys rather than girls. Her idea of a good time was to ride horseback or fight with clubs called cudgels. As she grew up, her favorite spot became the Bear Garden, a rough place where bears were cruelly baited or forced to fight dogs. Many of its customers were thieves and other lowlifes; they became Moll's friends and associates.

Although she loved the bloodthirsty spectacle of the Bear Garden, Moll was a pet fancier. She had many dogs that followed her around town, as did her pet monkey and several parrots.

Moll began working while still a child, but she didn't have a 9 to 5 job. Moll Frith apprenticed as a purse-snatcher. She had a real knack for it, too, as her fellow crooks at the Bear Garden appreciatively noticed. Soon the public (and the police) began to call her "Moll Cutpurse."

Now, you and I might think that a purse-snatcher would be a quiet and sneaky sort of person. But Moll was just the opposite. From childhood on, she sported boots, a leather doublet or vest,

THE NIP AND THE FOIST

Muggers and purse-snatchers in Renaissance England robbed their victims with "the nip." A thief performing this maneuver would spot someone with a purse heavy with coins, and simply split its bottom open. If the crime was well done, the victim didn't know or feel the loss until the "nipper" was well down the street.

Moll and other cutpurses preferred a more demanding technique called "the foist." To steal using the foist, Moll needed an eagle eye to see where her victim's "bung" or valuables were, steel nerves to approach the victim closely, and a feather touch to dive into the pocket or purse without being caught.

GANGSTA RAP IN OLD ENGLAND

"It's time to dead-lurk a crib," the Roaring Girle might announce to her pals. In thieves' lingo, she was saying "Let's rob a house while the folks are at church." When she bragged "I pitched a snide, and later I rattled the tats," she was telling people, "I passed some counterfeit coins—then I used phony dice in a card game." As you can see, a rich gangsta rap existed in Moll's England, hundreds of years before rappers in the United States climbed the charts. Slang words she used are still around today. When we say "Dibs on that pie!" we're using a word from that era.

and big breeches called galligaskins, like the men wore. She loved to laugh and play practical jokes. She proved to be a natural with the sword and the dagger. Her behavior won her yet another tag: people started calling her "Roaring Girle."

Growing up in London's criminal underworld as she did, Moll soon took up other bad habits. She grew fond of smoking a meerschaum pipe, and carried it everywhere. She swore a blue streak. Her drinking habits made her a favorite patron of taverns like the Globe and the Devil.

Once she had mastered thievery, this lightfingered extrovert graduated to bigger crimes. She began to burgle, or break into houses, and she learned how to fence (not the swordfighting kind, but getting money by selling stolen goods).

Moll Cutpurse was more clever than most crooks; she had organizational skills. Little by little, she set up her own fencing operation. By the time she was an adult she ruled London's underworld. Every day her gangs worked the city. Through her series of "offices" and "shops" in the teeming slums, Molly fenced thousands of pounds worth of goods that her gangs brought in. In fact, well-to-do people often came to her "stores" to see if they could buy back items that had been stolen from them!

Well-known as Moll became, she wasn't feared but admired. Londoners thought of her as their special celebrity. Needless to say, the police fumed. By now Moll Frith was getting wealthy. Very wealthy.

That didn't mean she was above the law. She ended up in prison a number of times. Even when she was not in London's Newgate Prison, Moll used to visit. On Sundays she would bring food to her mates in lockup. These and other heart-of-gold acts made Moll a legend.

In 1611, Moll appeared on the English stage, playing herself in "The Roaring Girle," although at that time women were forbidden to act, even in the female roles. As she stomped around in her male getup, singing a few off-color songs and strumming a lute, she brought down the house.

Criminals sometimes change their ways, especially as they grow older. Not Moll Frith. When a bloody civil war broke out in England between the royalists (those supporting King Charles I) and the Parliamentarians and rebels like Oliver Cromwell, all England took sides. Moll favored the royalists. To help their cause she became a highwaywoman, robbing stagecoaches and knocking off partisans of the rebel group. Once she attacked a Parliamentary General named Fairfax. She stopped his coach and entourage, shouting "Stand and deliver!" To speed up the general's response time, she shot him in the arm, killed two of his horses, and relieved him of a substantial amount of gold.

The Parliamentarian rebels were outraged. They put out an all-points bulletin and captured Moll Frith. "We've got her dead to rights!" they chortled, as they dragged her off to Newgate prison. Things looked bleak for Moll. She was sentenced to be hanged.

Not one to fold under pressure, Moll coolly contacted a colleague. She felt certain the officials would respond to a bribe. And indeed they did. For 2,000 English pounds (a small fortune today), Moll got out of prison and punishment.

For seventy-odd years, until she died of a stomach ailment, Moll Frith was London's favorite crook. A royal booster to the last, Moll left twenty English pounds in her will to "celebrate the restoration of King Charles II to his kingdom"—an event she missed seeing by one year.

Part Four

SPAIN
AND
PORTUGAL

ON THE IBERIAN *peninsula, the Renaissance was an age of exploration, personified by leaders like Queen Isabella, whose desire for gold and spices would lead Spain and its competitor, Portugal, to exploit the New World. At home the rulers of Spain and Portugal also persecuted some of their finer citizens, including the likes of philanthropist Gracia Mendes, and expelled the Jews and the Moors from their lands.*

Isabella of Castile

(1 4 5 1 - 1 5 0 4)

With her long chestnut hair gleaming with red highlights, Isabella looked all girl, demure and soft. Throughout her life she spoke in low tones, deferred to men, and kept her hands busy doing beautiful needlework. But Isabel was flinty hard, as tough as the rocky soil of her beloved kingdom of Castile, named for the *castillos* or castles that dotted its stark Spanish landscape.

Maybe Isabella was born that way. More likely, she was toughened by the unhappy events of her childhood. To cope, Isabella became a devout—some might even say fanatical—Catholic.

When she was around four, the princess lost her father—and her home. Her older half-brother Henry took the throne of Castile, then promptly banished Isabella, her baby brother Alfonso, and their mother to a small rundown place in Arévalo, near Ávila.

At first, Isabella went to school with the nuns of Santa Ana Convent. Later, when Alfonso was old enough, the two were tutored together at home. Isabella liked reading, writing, and music; she loved to paint delicate letters and figures on parchment, an art called illumination.

But the biggest lesson she learned was that treachery was everywhere. Her mother, often seriously ill with what sounds like the condition we'd now call depression, wasn't much support. Her half-brother the king and the people around him were evil and corrupt; they used threats, imprisonment, and dirty tricks to get their way.

The only friends Isabella could count on were her brother Alfonso and her childhood friend Beatriz de Bobadilla, the daughter of the castle-keeper. Beatriz's father gave each of them a pony and riding lessons when Isabella was six. Whenever they could, the three children would gallop across the flat countryside together. It was probably the only time Isabella felt happy and safe.

As a teenager, Isabella was looked at as a political pawn. Pressured to marry one of the worst scoundrels connected with the court, Isabella prayed for deliverance. And it came! On his way to wed the princess, the groom had an attack of quinsy (a bad form of tonsilitis), choked, and died.

The next year, a group of wellborn rebels hatched a plot to oust King Henry from the throne. Isabella's brother Alfonso, presented as a possible king, ended up as an innocent victim of the coup. When he died of suspicious causes, Isabella ran as fast as she could to the Convent of Santa Ana in Ávila. There she would be safe, she thought.

Soon the rebels came knocking on the convent door. They asked for an audience with the young princess. She agreed to see them, but only through the elaborate iron bars of the convent. "We want you to take the crown of Castile," they said. "We'll be loyal to you, not to your older brother Henry."

Isabella was intelligent enough to see a trap in the prize being offered. She shook her head. Her mouth was firm. "Henry is the lawful king of Castile. If I should gain the throne by disobedience to him, how could I blame anyone who might raise his hand in disobedience to me?"

"But Castile faces ruin," the group pleaded with her. She stayed inside the convent, unmoved. Four months later, the rebel leaders met with the king and signed a treaty with him. Isabella was present that warm September day in 1468 for the signing. In the treaty the king agreed to recognize Isabella as his legal heir, and awarded her seven cities, including her hometown, Ávila. Not only that, Henry had to promise that he would never force Isabella to marry against her wishes.

Henry didn't care for his sister's choice of a bridegroom. Ignoring her brother's arguments and the intrigues that swirled about her, Isabella chose to marry her second cousin Fernando. A year younger and an inch or two shorter than Isabella, he was the good-looking heir to the kingdom of Aragon, the fertile and rich province next to Castile. She knew two things: an alliance with Fernando would link their lands of Castile and Aragon into one united kingdom, a kingdom that after her lifetime would be known as Spain. And she honestly loved him. She and Fernando would become the most successful royal marriage of true partners that the world had ever seen.

When Henry died in 1474, Isabella acted swiftly to take the crown of Castile. By 1479, Isabella and Fernando were busy raising a family of five children, four girls and a boy. Even when pregnant or a new mom, Isabella stayed busy with affairs of state—and she wasn't just paper-shuffling. She worried over Spain as she did over her children. Under her half-brother's rule many nobles had set up their own small "kingdoms," ruling from castles in feudal

SPAIN'S FEMALE RENAISSANCE

Much of Queen Isabella's education came later in life, when she was a grown woman. In fact, she studied alongside her daughters Juana, Catherine, and Margaret! The queen's favorite teachers were women too: Bea Galindo, a professor from the University of Salamanca in northern Spain, whose nickname was La Latina; and Francisca de Lebrija, a shining light at the University of Alcalá near Madrid. They taught classical philosophy, literature, Latin, and Greek to the royal mother and daughters. Isabella and Juana both did well in their studies. But Isabella's daughter Catherine, who grew up to marry England's Henry the Eighth, was revered as a "learned lady" by Erasmus and other intellectuals of the day.

splendor. To restore royal authority Isabella crisscrossed the country on horseback, going here to inspire her troops by leading an army and there to lead the beginning of a city siege.

But there was still more to do, Isabella felt. Beginning about 1480, she and her husband decided on an even more difficult and dazzling goal: religious unity for Spain. They would expel the Moors—the Moslems who'd peacefully held much of the land for seven centuries. They would make all of Spain Catholic! The pope cheered the couple on, calling them "the athletes of Christ." For Isabella the War of Reconquest became a personal crusade. For more than ten years, the royal couple led the way into battle.

While Fernando concentrated on military tactics and troop movements, Isabella organized food supplies and improved roads so that cannons could travel on them. She put together a supply train that might have been in the *Guinness Book of World Records:* it included 80,000 pack mules! A caring woman, she set up the "Queen's Hospital," an early ambulance unit that traveled from one battlefield to another, its big tents a welcome sight to wounded soldiers.

As the years passed, the Moors were pushed further south. Nearly every month the queen saw the release of more Spanish prisoners, long held captive by the Moors during the 12-year-long struggle. On the sixth of January, 1492, the two monarchs won the War of Reconquest and rode victorious into Granada, the last Moorish stronghold.

Next, spurred on by their religious advisors, Isabella and Fernando issued an order to every Jew: convert to Catholicism or leave. Their Edict of Explusion said: "We order all Jews from all walks of life throughout the country to leave by July of this year. If

THE INQUISITION—
SPAIN'S BLACK MARK

In 1478, Isabella and Fernando set up the Spanish Inquisition, an organization employing thousands of secret agents. The inquisitors had almost unlimited legal powers to detain, torture, punish, and kill Jews, Moors, and people suspected of being witches or religious heretics.

Although Spain was far from the only country in Europe to set up an Inquisition, it was one of the busiest—and files on over 44,000 trials for heresy still exist!

it so happens that they come back or pass through our country, the penalty will be death and the confiscation of all their belongings will be ordered."

After Isabella and her husband signed this order, hundreds of thousands of Jews fled, going wherever they were accepted, like the Ottoman Empire (today's Turkey). This "racial and religious purity" policy didn't get the attention it deserved in the history books, possibly because it took place at the very same time and place as a more famous event: the expedition of Christopher Columbus.

King Fernando didn't think much of Columbus's proposal to find a passage to India and the Far East. But Queen Isabella put her money and her faith in the explorer, who set off with a fleet of three ships from southern Spain on August third. Instead of India, Columbus found a New World—new to Europeans, that is.

In 1504, Isabel died at age 53. Although this remarkable and

strong-willed woman had made possible the exploration of a New World, her plans for the immediate future of Spain failed. Her son, the heir apparent, died young. The rich prize of the Spanish throne passed to Isabella's daughter Juana, who went insane, and then to Isabella's grandson Charles. He inherited a Catholic Spain with its feet in both the Old and New Worlds. But not for long. Instead of a world empire, Charles witnessed the rise of a vibrant new religion called Protestantism. Isabella and Fernando's vision of a glorious all-Catholic Old and New World passed into history.

A 15TH-CENTURY "SPICE GIRL"

Queen Isabella funded Columbus's explorations partly because he promised to open up the spice trade to Spain. Spices from the east were costly, rare, and very popular in Europe, so those who controlled the spice trade could make a lot of money. Many of Christopher Columbus's promises didn't come true. He found very little gold; worse yet, he didn't find any rich sources of spices. On Haiti, Columbus did find a new variety of pepper—but that was it. The biggest hit was one lone pineapple that Columbus found in 1493.

Gracia Mendes Nasi

(A B O U T   1 5 1 0   -   1 5 6 9)

To the Christian citizens in Spain and Portugal, her name was Beatriz de Luna. To her family and a close circle of Jewish friends, her name was Gracia (the equivalent of the Hebrew name Hannah) Miguez Nasi. But her true name could just as well have been "courage."

During her 59 years of life, Gracia did many brave things. Perhaps the gutsiest was the "underground railroad" to freedom that she organized and helped. She put together this secret circuit to freedom for Jews fleeing persecution from Christians.

Gracia's story begins in Portugal, where she was born about 1510. Originally from Spain, the wealthy Nasi family had been pushed out, probably in the dark years around 1492 when Queen Isabella and King Fernando decreed that all Jews must leave that country.

Like thousands of others, the Nasi family settled in Lisbon, hoping to live in peace. In 1497 a new crisis arose. A princess of the Spanish royal family agreed to marry King Manoel of Portugal. The marriage deal, however, came with a big string attached. "You must purify your country as we have ours!" the princess and her family demanded. "Expel the Jews!"

King Manoel didn't want to lose the wealth and wisdom of his Jewish community; his solution was to forcibly convert the Jews. Families like the Nasis had to live double lives, trying to look like "good Christians" while remaining secretly true to their faith and culture. Sometimes answering to "Gracia," sometimes to "Beatriz," the little girl grew up in this strange fashion, surrounded by loving family members in the midst of a larger community filled with fear and treachery.

INSTANT CHRISTIANS

King Manoel didn't want to lose his Jewish population; rather, he wanted to erase their culture and make them into New Christians. To do this, he fixed on a cruel scheme: on March 19, 1497, he gave an order to all Jewish parents in Portugal: "You must bring every child of yours between four and fourteen to be baptized on Sunday! After the baptism, they'll be brought up by another family, so that they're certain to become good Christians." Then he ordered some 20,000 Jewish adults to be rounded up and held in miserable camps at the port of Lisbon. While they awaited ships to take them into exile, the Jews were psychologically tortured. Threatened with slavery or death, many converted. Others refused, but received "conversion" anyway—a few hasty words and a handful of Holy Water thrown over them from a distance. Only a handful of Jews actually got shipped to North Africa. The rest remained in Portugal, unwilling and frightened Christians in name—but not in spirit.

In spite of political upheavals Gracia's family was well-to-do. Her older brother even became the official doctor to the royal family.

When she was 18 or so, Gracia made a wonderful marriage to a rich fellow named Francisco Mendes. He and his younger brother Diogo were hotshots in the international business world who had made incredible profits buying and selling jewels and rare spices.

Francisco made an equally great match when he married Gracia. She was a striking woman with gleaming dark hair and fine compassionate eyes. Soon her husband learned that she was more than a mere beauty. She understood finance and quickly took an active part in his world of international business. The two found that they were soul mates in other ways as well. Both had a strong sense of pride in being Jewish, along with the courage to reach out to other Jews in worse circumstances. They took big risks. It's now thought that Francisco may have been one of Lisbon's religious leaders—he might even have been a rabbi.

Working with Francisco and Diogo, Gracia helped make the Mendes brothers' empire even richer and more far-flung. They opened more offices in England and Italy. Then personal disaster struck; Francisco died in 1536. Gracia was dazed by grief. Barely 26, she had a two-year-old daughter and two of her brother's children to bring up alone.

That same year, the Catholic Church ordered the Portuguese to set up an Office of the Inquisition, just as had been done in Spain. Government officials began to hunt down New Christians who secretly practiced Judaism—they were even forbidden to emigrate to any non-Christian lands.

Gracia looked around at her situation and made a decision. Francisco had left half of the family fortune to her to administer; the other half was with her brother-in-law. She decided to resettle in Antwerp, the Belgian city that was the heart of the Mendes business. Luckily, New Christians were still allowed to travel to Antwerp and some other northern cities.

The New York of its time, Antwerp dazzled the eye—and the nose. The spice fleet of Portugal filled Antwerp's harbor, its cargo sending scents along the grey cobblestone streets: the sharp smell of pepper, the sweet scent of cloves, the flowered aroma of spikenard, the breath-catching odor of camphor. Gracia's brother-in-law Diogo was thought of as the Spice King of Europe. He monopolized the pepper trade, and more than one king depended on him for financing.

The sharp-eyed young widow took to this environment. She began to work closely with him in all aspects of the business and family affairs. With Gracia's encouragement, Diogo married her sister Brianda.

Antwerp was freer than Portugal, but it was no picnic for Jews, Gracia soon saw. It was governed by Spanish royal rulers. At her mansion, she and others in the growing community of secret Jews got together for prayer and kept as many religious traditions as they dared. They also had to attend Mass and take part in other Catholic rituals.

With their resources, Gracia and her brother-in-law could have traveled wherever they liked, living around the world. They could have settled in faraway lands where their religion was not such an issue. But they did not—not for many years, anyway. Why? Because they both saw that they could do more good for their fellow Jews by remaining in Antwerp, a city that became a key stop on the underground railroad established by Gracia and Diogo. For Jews fleeing Spain or Portugal, Antwerp was the first stop on the way to freedom further south and east, in Italy and the Ottoman Empire (today's Turkey).

Gracia and Diogo jumped in to solve the refugees' problems. They set up their own elaborate spy organization. They had their own agents on the spice ships, who warned Jews hiding aboard when it was safe to disembark, and where it was safe to go. With their banking resources, Gracia and Diogo provided secret ways for Jews to get funds and property out of their home countries. On the long, complicated journey, these two even had "travel agents" along the way, to make sure that Jewish refugees did not fall into the wrong hands!

Even for the rich Mendes clan, life in Antwerp began to get harsher as the years rolled by and the Inquisition efforts became fiercer. Gracia talked earnestly to Diogo, saying, "We have to leave soon!"

But time ran out for Diogo; he died in the winter of 1542. In his will, he acknowledged Gracia as the person most capable of carrying on. She now took the reins of a business and family fortune that was one of the largest in Europe. Her nephew Joao became her right-hand man; later he became her son-in-law as well.

Gracia nimbly kept one step ahead of the greedy Inquisition officials. On a supposed "getaway" trip to a spa, she and the women in her family pulled up stakes and got safely to Venice (considered a tolerant regime), carrying most of the company assets in the portable form of jewels. For some years their mansion in Venice was a clearinghouse for Jews. Then the Venetians got greedy and intolerant in their turn. Wearily, the family moved on—this time, to Ferrara, Italy.

In 1553, Gracia finally found a haven that would remain safe. The destination? The Ottoman Empire and its capital, Constantinople. Her huge entourage of family, servants, and baggage took six months to reach Constantinople. Once there, the nonstop traveler, now 44 years old, entered the ancient city gates with a queenly splash. The admiring Turks saw a handsome

AN ENTRY FIT FOR A QUEEN: GRACIA ARRIVES IN CONSTANTINOPLE.

woman, the centerpiece of her own parade: four beautiful coaches, pulled by horses and flanked by 36 bodyguards in uniform.

Once settled in a palace overlooking the blue Bosphorus Sea, Gracia Mendes plunged into charitable work full-time, leaving business operations to her nephew. She built hospitals and synagogues. She subsidized schools and Hebrew-language printers. She supported the work of scholars and writers. She paid ransoms for countless Jews held hostage in hostile places. Gracia helped people on a one-to-one basis, too. Every single day at her home, eighty poor Jews sat down to lunch at her table.

A philanthropist for years, Gracia eventually became interested in Israel, the original homeland of the Jews. In her day, the land of Palestine was owned by the Ottoman Turks. She began to think that Jews belonged there more than any other place. The last project Gracia ever took on was to persuade the Sultan to let her pay a huge amount of money in taxes for Tiberias, a small city on the Sea of Galilee. Her plan? To set up a colony of 60,000 Jews there.

This time, Gracia also had a personal motive. She longed to

give her beloved husband Francisco a precious gift: a place for his bones to rest for eternity in the Holy Land of the Jews. And she got it. In 1559, she had his remains taken all the way from Lisbon to Tiberias, where they still rest today.

Perhaps Gracia's plan to return to Zion came too early. The first colony of 700 Jews, refugees from

Italy, did get to Tiberias but the colony eventually faltered, partly because of the climate and conditions. Gracia had built a house in Tiberias and was planning to go there, but judging from the fragmentary records of the day, she died in the summer of 1569, before she could set sail for the Holy Land. Nevertheless, her grand dream is still remembered and cherished by those who live in Israel.

Part Five

THE NEW WORLD

SPANISH AND PORTUGUESE *Old World culture spread to the New World, mixing with the societies that were already there, and at times dominating them. The aggressive invaders included women, like Basque outlaw and soldier of fortune Catalina de Erauso. A new hybrid culture soon developed in Mexico, Central America, and South America. Colorful New World women like Malinali, advisor and translator for the Spanish conquerors, and Juana de la Cruz, the outspoken philosopher-nun of Mexico, became important in these new societies.*

CHAPTER 13

Malinali of Mexico

(ABOUT 1505 - 1551)

E ven as a girl, Malinali could think and talk on her feet. Born around 1505 in a Mayan village on the north end of the Yucatán peninsula of what is now Mexico, she grew up to become a multilingual translator, strategist, and cultural advisor—the key player in one of the most important encounters between the Spanish conquerors of the Old World and the indigenous native peoples of the New World.

The first chapter of her life was pretty depressing, however. After her father died her mother remarried, then sold Malinali to a neighboring tribe as a slave. Barely in her teens, the new slave ended up in Xicalongo with another Mayan tribe. Later she was sold again, this time to the chief of Tabasco. Moving as she did around this great trading area of southern Mexico, Malinali first learned one Mayan dialect, then another. Eventually she also mastered Nahuatl, the language of the Aztecs. Fiercest of the people of old Mexico, the Aztecs kept everyone else in a state of terror, ruling from their capital city of Tenochtitlán.

THEIR BREECHES LOOKED LIKE TUTUS, BUT THE CONQUISTADORS WERE AS TOUGH AS NAILS.

When she reached her teens, Malinali was destined for her most fateful change of hands yet. On a day in March of 1519, ten shiploads of Spanish *conquistadores* (conquerors) led by Captain Hernán Cortés arrived on the shores of Yucatán. They immediately met resistance. In a clash, the *conquistadores* killed about a thousand natives.

The local chiefs made a peace offering to the Spaniards. In addition to gold jewelry, quilted cloth, and masks, the chiefs offered the strange men in shiny metal skins a special gift: twenty young female slaves.

One of the slaves was Malinali. With her long black hair and her confident air, she was a standout. As Bernal Díaz, one of the Spanish soldiers with Cortés, later noted in his journal, "She was good looking and intelligent and without embarrassment. . . ."

Before they did much else, the strange white men conducted a ceremony. They put up a large wooden pole on the beach, and they set up a smaller pole as a crossbar. Then they performed a rite they called "baptism." One by one, the women were baptized. When Malinali's turn came, she was given a new name. "You are now Doña Marina," Captain Cortés said, as he sprinkled drops of water on her head.

Cortés liked the looks of Malinali. Soon, however, he learned that she had something more valuable than looks and more precious than the gold the Spaniards sought. The teenager could speak the many languages of old Mexico. That meant she could communicate with one of the Spaniards on the expedition, who knew a Mayan tongue.

In an instant, she rose from the status of slave to the key role of interpreter. Malinali could parley with different local tribes, and she was a treasure-house of knowledge about the Aztec and Mayan cultures. Not only that, but she had been mistreated by her own people. Cortés was gleeful. The odds had been against him and his tiny band in this land, but now he had a secret weapon to conquer Mexico!

With her quick wits, Malinali saw that she would have even more power and credibility with these strangers if she spoke Spanish, too. So she worked hard and soon learned the white man's tongue.

Quickly she became a confidant and advisor to Cortés as well as the main translator for all negotiations. Further proving her worth, Malinali even uncovered a plot on Cortés's life.

As the band of Spaniards pushed on to Tenochtitlán (located

where Mexico City is today), the tireless translator helped in many ways. She drew maps of the countryside. She showed the Spaniards how to treat sickness and wounds with local plants. She acted as a public relations person, convincing local tribes that they should make peace pronto with these godlike creatures. She filled the Spaniards in on the tactics and weapons that Aztecs and other Indians used in war.

Malinali had great common sense. At her first encounter with them, she too thought that the tall strangers might be gods. She learned differently. Despite their frightening weapons—the great animals called "horses" and the smoking tubes they called "muskets"—they could be hurt. After a fierce battle, she saw that they could die just as the Aztecs did. Shrewdly, she told Cortés: "Make sure you bury or take away the bodies of your dead. That way, the locals will still believe you are the gods returned."

When the Spaniards arrived at the Aztec capital, the sight of

A MYTH CONQUERED MEXICO'S MILLIONS

Just as Christians believe in a Messiah who will someday return to earth, various Indian tribes of old Mexico believed that their god Quetzalcoatl would return over the water in a canoe from the east, in the form of a white and bearded god. When a bearded Cortés and other male soldiers with beards arrived in ships like giant canoes, it seemed to the Aztecs and other Indians that Quetzalcoatl's promise had come true. When Malinali told the white men about the legend, the Spaniards were able to make maximum advantage of the reverence and fear they inspired.

its five linked lakes and waterways, its clean streets bright with floating gardens, and its tall pyramids astounded them. Soon Malinali and Cortés were deep in negotiations with Montezuma, the famed leader of the Aztecs. Smart as he was, Montezuma was no match for the cunning of Malinali and Cortés. Soon Malinali had persuaded the Aztec leader to invite the Spanish band into the city as his guests.

For months, an uneasy Montezuma had been hearing about the gods who had arrived on the shores of his land. A religious man, he was taking no chances. Better to welcome them, he thought.

With Malinali's help, Cortés was able to play on Montezuma's fears. He demanded gold; the Aztec leader gave him roomsful of it. Once Cortés had the gold, the Spaniards took Montezuma captive. For months, the band held millions of Aztecs at bay with their hostage. Instead of blaming the intruders, the Aztecs got angry at their leader. Finally, the Spaniards brought Montezuma up on a flat rooftop so that everyone could see that he was all right. A riot broke out. In the stone-throwing that followed, Montezuma took a rock in the head from an angry citizen and died three days later. In the battle that followed, the Aztecs drove the Spaniards from their city. On that bloody night, many fell. Others of the Cortés band drowned—weighed down with the gold they tried to carry off. Malinali and Cortés, however, escaped.

Little by little Hernán Cortés regrouped, getting troop reinforcements from Cuba for a final assault. The Spaniards laid siege to the great Aztec capital, cutting off its supplies of food and water.

By now, a horrible "secret weapon" was at work—one that the Spaniards didn't even know they possessed. Inside the city and throughout the Valley of Mexico, an epidemic of smallpox (and

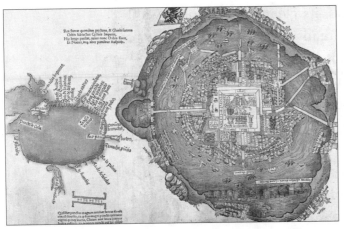

THE AZTEC CAPITAL OF TENOCHTITLÁN WAS TEN TIMES THE SIZE OF ANY CITY IN SPAIN AT THE TIME.

possibly another of measles) spread, brought by the Europeans. Aztecs, young and old, rich and poor, died by the millions because they had no immunity to these new diseases. On August 13, 1521, the great city of Tenochtitlán fell to the Spaniards. They found a pathetic remnant of the population—as few as 10 percent of the people had survived.

For her key role in the Spanish conquest of Mexico, Malinali won gifts of land in Jilotepec and gold from Cortés. She also won her freedom. (Ironically, one of Cortés's gifts to her was a set of slaves of her own!) She also had a child, who was Cortés's son. She named him Martín.

Through her work, many Indians and Spaniards alike came to respect her. When she became powerful enough, she insisted on being called by yet another name: Malintzín. Only Aztec nobles could put the suffix "tzín" on the end of their names—it was a mark of their high standing. The Spaniards spelled her honorary name phonetically. On paper, it became "Malinche"—a name often used for her today.

Not everyone thought highly of Malinali. A number of Aztecs and Mayans hated her. Even today, some Mexicans call her a traitor to her race. Looking at this intelligent and valiant woman, who was tossed aside by three different tribes, it's hard to blame this survivor for siding with the Spaniards. They were the only ones who appreciated her.

Catalina de Erauso

(A B O U T   1 5 8 5   -   1 6 5 0)

Like many another sixteenth century girl baby born to a typical Basque family of northern Spain, Catalina had dark hair, dark eyes, and plump cheeks. And she was treated like just another girl in the de Erauso family. "We have other daughters to think about. When Catalina is four, we shall dedicate her to God," decided her parents. Little did they know how outrageous little Catalina would become.

From the outset, Catalina was a square peg in a round hole at the Dominican convent of San Sebastián el Antiguo. Even though the head of the convent was her aunt Ursula, the religious life did not run in her blood. She had a rebellious streak a mile wide and often fought with the other novices.

When she was 15, the year in which she would have taken her final vows to become a nun, she quarreled with an older nun who physically punished her.

Catalina had had it. As she later wrote, "She was a big, robust woman, I was but a girl—and when she beat me, I felt it." Still smarting from her mistreatment, Catalina looked for an opportunity to steal the keys to the convent. On the morning of March 18 in the year 1600, she escaped from the nunnery, taking nothing but a few stolen coins and her free spirit. For three days, Catalina hid in a chestnut grove near the convent, getting by on a few herbs she found to eat. Catalina might have been a tomboy, but like all young Spanish girls she'd been taught to sew. First she made a pair of pants out of her one garment of blue wool. Then she created a doublet (we'd call it a jacket) and long hose out of her green petticoat. She whacked her wavy black hair into a pageboy, trimmed her bangs, and tossed her tresses away, along with any telltale remnants of her nun's habit.

Catalina had a strong chin, bold eyebrows, and a rather long and imposing nose. Her shoulders were big, her body sturdy. Now dressed like any young man of the day, she found easy acceptance as a boy.

She might have been a 15-year-old fresh out of the convent, but Catalina was no angel. She picked up jobs and won people's confidence—then "supplemented" her salary as a servant or page by stealing from her employers before moving on! Once she got into a rock fight with the local boys and spent a month in jail.

For three years Catalina bounced around Spain, having fun, getting into and out of scrapes, wearing a variety of nifty male garments, and never staying in one place too long. So complete was her transformation that at one point she had the nerve to stroll around her old home town of San Sebastián. She even went to Catholic mass back at her old convent! There her own mother saw her in the crowd—but didn't recognize her.

At length, she wandered toward southern Spain. In Sanlúcar, near Sevilla, she got hired for one of the toughest jobs on board ship: cabin boy. The ship was a Spanish galleon, headed for South America in the New World. Another coincidence—the ship was owned by one of her uncles. Like other family members, he failed to recognize her.

One night shortly after arrival on the shores of South America, Catalina jumped ship, lifting 500 pesos of her uncle's money before she melted into the night.

Calling herself by various male names, Catalina roamed Central and South America, from Panama to the "wild west" Andean highlands of Peru to the long land of Chile. She joined the

TRANSGENDER SOLDIERS OF FORTUNE

Between the centuries of 1500 and 1800, a surprising number of young women throughout Europe opted to take on male appearance and clothing. Many lived out their entire lives without anyone being the wiser. Most joined the military, serving on ships or in armies. Others became freelance soldiers of fortune—or outlaws, as Catalina was. We now have evidence about hundreds of women in the Netherlands, England, France, and other parts of Europe who lived transgendered lives.

Spanish army that conquered Chile, became a lieutenant, and served with valor. As tough as the leather vest and shiny metal armor she wore, Catalina survived shipwrecks, a stint as a prisoner of war, holdups, disease, and arrow wounds.

But she was an outlaw at heart. De Erauso couldn't get enough of gambling and card games. Her love of strong drink, combined with her always hot temper and her sharp tongue, often got her into knife fights, street brawls, and duels. She ended up killing at least a dozen men. For years she ran just ahead of the law. Several times she barely escaped hanging for one or another of her crimes.

Around 1619, when she was in her mid-thirties, her luck seemed to have run out. Sought by the police for armed robbery, murder, and other crimes, she found herself in a *Butch Cassidy*

A CASE OF MISTAKEN IDENTITY

The strangest murder Catalina ever committed happened in the army. As a lieutenant serving in Chile, she developed a close comradeship with a man who turned out to be her older brother Miguel, who was a captain. He didn't recognize his sister, but then he'd left home when she was two. One night, a drinking buddy asked her to act as a second in a duel he'd been challenged to. Catalina agreed. The dueling ground was dark as pitch. After both duelists had fallen, Catalina took up her sword. In the darkness, she and the other second parried and thrust. Catalina drove her sword into the man's chest, only to hear her own brother cry out. A friend to the end, he died without telling anyone who had delivered the fatal blow.

and the Sundance Kid–style battle with sheriffs in the Peruvian town of Guamanga. Wounded, she sought refuge in a nearby church.

Perhaps she was just tired of running. Perhaps the weight of her secret identity was too much. At any rate, Catalina confessed her whole story—and her female gender—to the bishop. He was amazed. He was even more astonished to learn that she had remained a virgin.

You'd think that Catalina de Erauso would spend the rest of her days in prison for her bad deeds. But people in both the New World and the Old viewed her case as extraordinary. The bishop said "I esteem you as one of the more remarkable people in this world," and contacted the pope with her story. She became a celebrity overnight. People trooped to see her at the convent of Santa Clara in Guamanga, where she remained for the time being. They began to call her "la Monja Alférez"—the "Lieutenant Nun."

Meanwhile, the bishop sent a letter to her old convent in San Sebastián to find out if Catalina had told the truth about not taking her final religious vows. If so, then she would be free to go. While she waited, Catalina lived in a Peruvian convent. It took two years and five months before the response came. To keep busy, she dictated her memoirs to a scribe during the long wait.

In 1624, Catalina finally returned to Spain. Big crowds turned up everywhere she went, trying to get a glimpse of the fabled Lieutenant Nun in male warrior's clothing. Eventually she made it to Madrid and got an audience with the King of Spain. She presented her memoirs, then hit him up for a pension. And she got 800 crowns a year, although as she remarked, "that was a little less than the sum I had asked for."

SOLDIER OF FORTUNE
CATALINA SURVIVED
WAR WOUNDS,
SHIPWRECK, AND
HOT ARMOR.

Catalina was on a roll now; she made the boat trip from Spain to Italy in 1626, where she kissed the feet of Pope Urban the Eighth and told him her story. Amazed as others had been, the pope granted her the right to live her life dressed in men's clothes. (He also gave Catalina a couple of timid reminders about leading an honest existence from that day forward, and not killing anyone else!)

Before her return to the New World, Catalina was honored by the cardinals of Rome and made an honorary Roman citizen. One of the cardinals tried to compliment her, saying that "her only fault was that she was a Spaniard." She replied, "With all due respect, your Holiness, that is my only virtue."

Catalina de Erauso made one more round trip between the Old and New Worlds; in 1630 she met with her sisters one last time, got her share of the family inheritance, and returned to Mexico. This time, she called herself Antonio de Erauso. The last reliable report of her in 1645 came from a friar, who saw her running a mule train, moving goods around Mexico. Strong, burned by the sun, a bit stout but wearing her silver dagger and sword, Catalina was still known in those parts as a person of courage and skill.

CHAPTER 15

Sor Juana de la Cruz

(1 6 5 1 - A P R I L   1 7 ,   1 6 9 5)

A t her christening on December 2, 1651, the little girl with the long name of Juana Inés de Asabaje Ramírez was described as a "daughter of the church"—an expression that meant that her parents weren't married. Her father, a poor Basque of good family, had come to Mexico to seek his fortune. Her mother Isabel was a criolla, born in Mexico of Spanish parents. Although well to do, she was one of eleven daughters. Perhaps the lack of a good dowry prevented Juana's parents from marrying.

Juana's father drifted away from the family early. She, her five sisters, and her mom lived with grandfather Ramírez on his hacienda at Nepantla. The hacienda had one glorious room that made a huge impression on Juana: her grandfather's library. (Books, especially imported ones, were as pricey as gold jewelry.)

Little Juana had big brown eyes, thick honey-colored hair that reached her waist, and small chubby hands. At three years old, she tagged after her sister María Josefa to school and told the teacher, "My mother wants me to have lessons in reading and writing, too."

Surprised, the teacher saw that the toddler could already hold a quill pen in her small hands. Soon she read and wrote better than most of the older kids.

As Juana grew, she heard grownups talk about the university in Mexico City, where people could learn science, mathematics, and other subjects. "Mamá!" she would say. "I want to go to *la universidad!*" When her mother said, "University is a place for men only, daughter," Juana would declare, "Then I shall go, dressed as a man!"

Juana never got to college. Instead, this fatherless girl tackled the job of educating herself. Working from her grandfather's library, she studied foreign languages, astronomy, biology, music, drawing, math, and painting. Eventually, she read every book in his library.

At age seven, she entered her first poem in a Corpus Christi festival. She won a precious prize: a book of her very own. The following year, Juana's mother said, "You're going to Mexico City to

CURLS FOR CREDIT

As a self-made student, Juana was very tough on herself. At times she would give herself a certain amount of time to master her lessons. If she didn't reach her goal, off came a length of her beautiful hair. (Hair was really the "crowning glory" for girls and women in that day and age—so chopping your locks was a real punishment!)

live with your aunt María and uncle Juan. They have money—they'll be able to help you more than I can."

Soon one of Juana's dreams came true: her aunt and uncle paid for a tutor to teach her Latin, the language used in the most important books of her day.

When she was about 13, more luck came to the thirsty young seeker of knowledge. A new Viceroy (the ruler) of Mexico took office. He and his well-educated wife, the Marquesa Laura, decided to bring a few deserving local children to court, give them a good education and teach them manners. Juana's aunt took her to meet the rulers. The competition was stiff, but Juana stood out.

"We'll make you a lady-in-waiting," they said. Marquesa Laura even gave Juana a special title. "We'll call you 'dearly beloved of the Señora Viceroy.'"

Because she already had a reputation as a child prodigy, Juana found herself the center of an unusual event that the Marquesa put together. She brought 40 professors together, all experts in their fields of science, math, literature, history, and religion. Their job? To give young Juana a public test of her knowledge. (Just imagine a "Special Jeopardy" round with one person being questioned by 40 experts!)

For the occasion, Marquesa Laura had a dress made for Juana, copied from the latest fashions in the Spanish court. The full skirt was peach brocade; the puffy satin sleeves were blue and laced with ribbons; around her middle Juana wore a black velvet bodice. In her hair Juana wore a gold hairclip trimmed with pearls and turquoise.

Nervous but poised, Juana faced the male scholars. Her answers showed she was equal to the task. The Viceroy later wrote,

"YOU HAVE TEN
SECONDS TO NAME
THE CAPITAL
CITIES OF THE
WORLD!"

"She handled herself like a royal galleon, defending itself against a horde of attacking canoes."

After this triumph, Juana's career would seem to be made. But we must remember that this was seventeenth-century Mexico—and Juana was not a woman of independent means. Painfully few women, no matter how bright and motivated, could pursue a career, much less the life of a scholar.

In 1667, Juana decided to enter a convent. Becoming a nun seemed the only way to pursue an independent life of the mind. The 17-year-old now adopted the name she would carry the rest of her life: Sor Juana de la Cruz (or Sister Joan of the Cross).

At the convent of San Jerónimo she had a two-story apartment with a window overlooking the Valley of Mexico and the

Popocatepetl Volcano. There was a room where she could have intellectual friends visit. Sor Juana could read and write and correspond with leading figures of her time. And best of all, she could collect books! In time, she put together a private library of more than 4,000 volumes—the largest collection ever seen in Mexico. Sor Juana also collected maps, musical instruments, and scientific paraphernalia, making her library a mini-museum!

A celebrated nun, she also wrote poetry, dramatic plays, even comedies. In the evenings, learned friends and famous visitors often came to the convent for music, plays, and poetry readings that Juana put together. Her friend and mentor Carlos de Sigüenza y Góngora gave her a course in study for the sciences; she in turn worked with him on his poetry.

Sor Juana also had religious duties at the convent—and some not so religious. She took care of the financial records, paid the bills, and handled the archives. Twice the nuns asked her to be their Mother Superior, but she refused.

Although she wasn't wealthy, Juana had many patrons and supporters. With these resources, she was finally able to help her own four sisters. They really needed it. Two sisters and their children had been abandoned by their husbands. Juana helped one sister buy a hacienda, gave the children educations, saw that they married well, and had respected careers.

One of the most productive years of Juana's active life may have been 1680. That year, she wrote more than one hundred poems. As Sor Juana became older, her daring mix of religious and worldly themes began to make some people uneasy. She was criticized by church superiors. In 1690, she got into a religious debate with a sly bishop. At the time, she thought that she was having a private exchange of opinions via letter. Instead, her tricky opponent plotted to bring her down by making their words public. (Like leaks to the press and the secret taping of telephone conversations in our time, this caused a storm of controversy in Juana's day.)

To answer his charges that she was selfish, insufficiently humble, and as a woman displayed "audacity" in her pursuit of a life of the mind, Juana wrote *La Respuesta* (The Answer). It took her three solid months. In it, she told of her life. She supported the rights of women, arguing that they were reasoning human beings and should have the right to be scholars if they wished.

Although Juana's *Answer* was not published until after her death, Juana felt that she'd defended her beliefs and her honor by writing it. Then she did an appalling thing: she dismantled her library, book by book. She sold everything, then donated the monies to the poor. From that moment on, Juana turned away from her life of the mind. She carried out her routine duties at the Convento San Jerónimo. That was all.

In 1695, when Juana was 47, plague hit Mexico City. Without a thought for her own safety, Juana went out into the streets, nursing those who needed it most. Day and night she bravely worked—until calamity hit. On April 17 of that year, Sor Juana de la Cruz died of the plague. At her funeral, attended by huge numbers of famous faces and humble admirers, her lifelong friend Carlos gave the eulogy for the woman whom he and the world called "*la Décima Musa*"—the Tenth Muse. Sor Juana is still thought of as Mexico's Muse today, and twice she has been honored on Mexican stamps.

N$ 1.80

MIGUEL DE CABRERA

TERCER CENTENARIO LUCTUOSO DE SOR JUANA INÉS DE LA CRUZ
TRES SIGLOS DE INMORTALIDAD
1695 - 1995
H. ORTÍZ   ROMO   MÉXICO

Servicio Postal Mexicano

SUGGESTED READING

ote: Most of the primary sources used to write these biographies are difficult to read, even for adults. The books below are suitable for motivated younger readers. Some are primary sources.

Adams, Jerome. *Notable Latin American Women.* (Jefferson, NC: McFarland & Company 1995).

Alic, Margaret. *Hypatia's Heritage.* (Boston: Beacon 1986).

Ashby, Ruth, et al. *Herstory: Women Who Changed the World.* (New York: Viking 1995). For young adults.

de Erauso, Catalina. *Lieutenant Nun.* (Boston: Beacon 1996).

Forbes, Malcolm. *Women Who Made a Difference.* (New York: Simon and Schuster 1990). For young adults.

Fraser, Antonia. *Warrior Queens.* (New York: Vintage Books 1988).

Greer, Germaine. *The Obstacle Race.* (New York: Farrar Straus & Giroux 1979).

Heller, Nancy. *Women Artists.* (New York: Abbeville 1987).

Henry, Sondra, and Emily Taitz. *Written Out of History: Jewish Foremothers.* (Sunnyside, NY: Biblio Press 1990).

Jackson, Guida. *Women Who Ruled.* (Santa Barbara, CA: ABC-Clio 1990).

Joan of Arc. *Joan of Arc in Her Own Words.* (Chappaqua, NY: Turtle Point Press 1996).

Keyes, Frances. *Land of Stones and Saints.* (New York: Doubleday 1957).

King, Margaret. *Women of the Renaissance.* (Chicago: U. of Chicago Press 1991).

Klausman, Ulrike, et al. *Women Pirates.* (Buffalo, NY: Black Rose Books 1997).

León, Vicki. *Uppity Women of the Renaissance.* (Berkeley, CA: Conari Press 1999).

Mackey, Joan and Kenneth. *Book of Women's Achievements.* (New York: Stein and Day 1976).

McCully, Emily A. *The Pirate Queen.* (New York: Putnam 1995). For children.

Newark, Tim. *Women Warriors.* (London: Blandford 1989).

Ogilvie, Marilyn. *Women in Science: Antiquity Through the 19th Century.* (Cambridge, MA: MIT Press 1993).

Partnow, Elaine, ed. *The Quotable Woman From Eve to 1799.* (New York: Facts on File 1985).

Raven, Susan, and Alison Weir. *Women of Achievement.* (New York: Harmony Books 1981).

Roth, Cecil. *The House of Nasi: Doña Gracia.* (Philadelphia: Jewish Publication Society 1948).

Sachar, Howard. *Farewell España.* (New York: Vintage Books 1994).

(Most of the dates here and throughout the book are approximate.)

A.D. 1400 - 1700

Joan of Arc: 1412–May 30, 1431
Isabella of Castile: 1451–1504
Vittoria Colonna: about 1490–Feb. 20, 1547

Margaret More Roper: 1505–1544
Malinali of Mexico: about 1505–1551
Gracia Mendes Nasi: about 1510–1569

Kenau Hasselaar: about 1526–1588
Grace O'Malley of Ireland: about 1530–1603
Elizabeth I of England: 1533–Mar. 24, 1603

Sophie Brahe: 1556–1643
Catalina de Erauso: about 1585–1650
Moll Frith: about 1589–1659

Christina of Sweden: 1626–1689
Elisabetta Sirani: 1638–Aug. 25, 1665
Sor Juana de la Cruz: 1651–April 17, 1695

OTHER OUTRAGEOUS WOMEN OF THE RENAISSANCE

If you'd like to learn more about other notable women of this age, you could start with the list below. Then check out the bibliography on pages 111–112 where you'll see an abundance of books, some of them even written by women of the times.

- **Katherine von Bora,** the hard-working wife of Martin Luther. In her earlier life as a German nun, she and her sisters at the convent wanted to become Lutherans. Not only did Luther help, but he and Katherine ended up as partners in a marriage where she kept the family going financially.

- **Aphra Amis Behn,** an English playwright and the first person in England to make a living as a writer. Adventurous world traveler Aphra also worked as a spy. When she didn't get paid, she got a surprise—a stay in debtors' prison.

- **Birgitta of Sweden,** a visionary (and now Sweden's patron saint) lived at the beginning of the Renaissance period. She married and had eight children before getting a religious calling. Among other deeds, she founded a monastery and wrote down more than 700 of her visions.

- **Marie le Jars de Gourney,** a self-taught Frenchwoman from a small village, corresponded for years with Michel de Montaigne, the most important philosopher of her day. After his death, this busy woman edited his work, did lecture tours, and became a feminist writer and an alchemist.

- **Cassandra Fedele of Venice,** one of the many brilliant female humanists of the Renaissance, gave recitals to big audiences by her teen years. Once she married, however, her intellectual activity stopped. When left a widow with no money, Cassandra became head of an orphanage and lived to be 93.

Stamp of Elisabetta Sirani's Mother and Child (pp. *x*, 20) copyright ©
1993 by U.S.P.S., all rights reserved; stamp of Sor Juana Inés de la Cruz
(pp. *x*, 110) courtesy of Servicio Postal Mexicano; portrait of Joan of Arc
entering Orléans (p. 6) courtesy of Archive Photos; portrait of Vittoria
Colonna (p. 11) © The British Museum, London; painting *Melpomene,
the Muse of Tragedy* (p. 18), by Elisabetta Sirani (Italian, 1638–1665), oil
on canvas $34\frac{1}{2}$" x 28", courtesy of The National Museum of Women,
Washington, D.C./Gift of Wallace and Wilhelmina Holladay; portrait of
Kenau Hasselaar (p. 29) courtesy of Hulton Getty/Liaison Agency; image
of Christina of Sweden (p. 39) courtesy of Archive Photos; portrait of Sir
Thomas More bidding his daughter farewell (p. 51) courtesy of Archive
Photos; portrait of Elizabeth I knighting Francis Drake (p. 56) courtesy of
Hulton Getty/Liaison Agency; image of Tenochtitlán (p. 98) courtesy
of Edward E. Ayer Collection/Newberry Library, Chicago; portrait of
Catalina de Erauso (p. 104) © The British Museum, London. We grate-
fully acknowledge permission to quote the poetry of Vittoria Colonna
(p. 12) from *Women Writers of the Renaissance and Reformation*, Love
Poems IV, by Katharina M. Wilson, transl. Joseph Gibaldi (Athens, Ga.:
University of Georgia Press, 1987).